Faith & Work

Rich in Good Deeds: A Biblical Response to Poverty by the Church and by Society, ed. Robert L. Plummer

Healthy and Wealthy? A Biblical-Theological Response to the Prosperity Gospel, ed. Robert L. Plummer

Healthy and Wealthy?
A Biblical-Theological Response to the Prosperity Gospel

Healthy and Wealthy?

A Biblical-Theological Response to the Prosperity Gospel

❦

Edited by Robert L. Plummer

Fontes

Healthy and Wealthy?
A Biblical-Theological Response to the Prosperity Gospel

Copyright © 2022 by Robert L. Plummer

ISBN-13: 978-1-948048-71-2 (paperback)

All rights reserved. No part of this publication may be reproduced, stored in a retrieval system, or transmitted in any form or by any means—electronic, mechanical, photocopy, recording, or any other—except for brief quotations in printed reviews, without the prior permission of the publisher.

Managing Editor: Jarrett Ford

Typeset by Monolateral in Minion 3, Ezra SIL SR, and Museo Sans.

Fontes Press
Dallas, TX
www.fontespress.com

Contents

Abbreviations ix

Contributors xiii

Preface xvii

1. An Evaluation of the Historical Apologetic against "Word-Faith Theology" 1
   Benjamin T. Cornish

2. Wealth and Poverty in Proverbs and Ecclesiastes 27
   James M. Hamilton Jr.

3. "Provided We Suffer with Him": A Pauline Theology of Suffering and the Prosperity Gospel 45
   Michael E. Pohlman

4. The Unique Temptations of Wealth and Poverty Over Time 61
   David S. Kotter

5. Wealth, Poverty, and the Heavenly City in John's Apocalypse 79
   Michael P. Naylor

6. How Shall We Sing the Prosperity Gospel's Song in an Evangelical Church? 95
   Matthew D. Westerholm

7. Possessions, Greed and the Christian Community: Interrogating the Prosperity Gospel in Africa in Light of Hebrews 13:1–6 121
   Abeneazer G. Urga

8. Conceptions of the Good Life in the Apostolic Era 135
   Todd A. Scacewater

9. "To Prosper" or צלח in Genesis 39 153
   Philip Suciadi Chia

Index 171

Abbreviations

1 En.	1 Enoch
11Q19	Temple Scroll[a]
1QM	Milḥamah *or* War Scroll
1QpHab	Pesher Habakkuk
2 En.	2 Enoch
3 Bar.	3 Baruch (Syriac Apocalypse)
4 Macc	4 Maccabees
4Q504	DibHam[a] (Dibre Hame'orot[a] [Words of the Luminaries[a]])
4QIsa[d]	4QIsaiah Pesherd
AB	Anchor Bible
ACCSOT	Ancient Christian Commentary on Scripture: Old Testament
Ant.	*Jewish Antiquities*
Ap.	*Apologia*
Apoc. Mos.	Apocalypse of Moses
Apoc. Sedr.	Apocalypse of Sedrach
ApOTC	Apollos Old Testament Commentary
Av.	*Aves*
BBR	*Bulletin for Biblical Research*
BDAG	Danker, Frederick W., Walter Bauer, William F. Arndt, and F. Wilbur Gingrich. *Greek-English Lexicon of the New Testament and Other Early Christian Literature.* 3rd ed. University of Chicago Press, 2000
BDB	Brown, Francis, S. R. Driver, and Charles A. Briggs. *A Hebrew and English Lexicon of the Old Testament*

BECNT	Baker Exegetical Commentary on the New Testament
CBQ	*Catholic Biblical Quarterly*
CH	*Church History*
Comp. Sol. Publ.	*Comparatio solonis et Publicolae*
ConcC	Concordia Commentary
CSCO	Corpus Scriptorum Christianorum Orientalium
Diatr.	*Diatribai* (*Dissertationes*)
Did.	Didache
Diog. Laert.	Diogenes Laërtius, *Lives of Eminent Philosophers*
Enn.	*Enneads*
Eth. nic.	*Ethica nicomachea*
Euthyd.	*Euthydemus*
Euthyphr.	*Euthyphro*
Fel.	*De felicitate* (*Or.* 51)
FOTL	Forms of the Old Testament Literature
Gorg.	*Gorgias*
Gymn.	*De gymnastica*
HALOT	*The Hebrew and Aramaic Lexicon of the Old Testament.* By Ludwig Koehler, Walter Baumgartner, and Johann J. Stamm. Translated and edited under the supervision of Mervyn E. J. Richardson. 4 vols. Brill, 1994–1999
HBT	*Horizons in Biblical Theology*
Hist.	*Historiae*
HRCS	Hatch, Edwin, and Henry A. Redpath. *Concordance to the Septuagint and Other Greek Versions of the Old Testament.* 2 vols. Clarendon, 1897. 2nd ed. Baker, 1998.
HTS	Harvard Theological Studies
IBC	Interpretation: A Bible Commentary for Teaching and Preaching
ICC	International Critical Commentary
Int	*Interpretation*
J.W.	Jewish War
JAAR	*Journal of the American Academy of Religion*
JBL	*Journal of Biblical Literature*
JSNT	*Journal for the Study of the New Testament*
JSNTSup	Journal for the Study of the New Testament Supplement Series

JSOTSup	Journal for the Study of the Old Testament Supplement Series
KEK	Kritisch-exegetischer Kommentar über das Neue Testament (Meyer-Kommentar)
LCL	Loeb Classical Library
Leg.	*Leges*
Let. Aris.	Letter of Aristeas
List	*Listening: Journal of Religion and Culture*
LNTS	The Library of New Testament Studies
LSJ	Liddell, Henry George, Robert Scott, and Henry Stuart Jones. *A Greek-English Lexicon*. 9th ed. with revised supplement. Clarendon, 1996
LXX	Septuagint
Med.	*Meditations*
NAC	New American Commentary
Neot	*Neotestamentica*
NICNT	New International Commentary on the New Testament
NICOT	New International Commentary on the Old Testament
NIDNTTE	*New International Dictionary of New Testament Theology and Exegesis*. Edited by Moisés Silva. 5 vols. Zondervan, 2014
NIGTC	New International Greek Testament Commentary
NovT	*Novum Testamentum*
NSBT	New Studies in Biblical Theology
NT	New Testament
OBT	Overtures to Biblical Theology
Opif.	*De opificio mundi*
OT	Old Testament
Phaedr.	*Phaedrus*
Phileb.	*Philebus*
Phoen.	*Phoenissae*
Plut.	*Plutus*
Pneuma	*Pneuma: Journal for the Society of Pentecostal Studies*
PNTC	Pillar New Testament Commentaries
Pol.	*Politica*
Ps.-Philo	Pseudo-Philo (Liber antiquitatum biblicarum)
Pss. Sol.	Psalms of Solomon

SBLDS	Society of Biblical Literature Dissertation Series
SBT	Studies in Biblical Theology
Sib. Or.	Sibylline Oracles
SNTSMS	Society for New Testament Studies Monograph Series
ST	*Studia Theologica*
T. Job.	Testament of Job
TDNT	*Theological Dictionary of the New Testament.* Edited by Gerhard Kittel and Gerhard Friedrich. Translated by Geoffrey W. Bromiley. 10 vols. Eerdmans, 1964–1976
TNTC	Tyndale New Testament Commentaries
Tob	Tobit
Tro.	*Troades*
TynBul	*Tyndale Bulletin*
WBC	Word Biblical Commentary
Wis	Wisdom of Solomon
WUNT	Wissenschaftliche Untersuchungen zum Neuen Testament
WW	*Word and World*
ZECNT	Zondervan Exegetical Commentary on the New Testament
ZNW	*Zeitschrift für die Neutestamentliche Wissenschaft und die Kunde der alteren Kirche*

Contributors

PHILIP SUCIADI CHIA, D.Th., Ph.D., is a director of doctoral studies at Evangelical Theological Seminary of Indonesia and an adjunct professor at Reformed Theological Seminary of Indonesia. In addition to books for Christianity in Indonesia, he has also published articles in *Biblical Theological Bulletin, Journal of Research on Christian Education, Sophia, Verbum et Ecclesia,* and *Transformation: An International Journal of Holistic Mission Studies.*

BENJAMIN T. CORNISH is a Ph.D. candidate in World Religions at the Southern Baptist Theological Seminary in Louisville, KY. He is also the President of Teaching Truth International, a missions organization that creates and teaches biblical and theological curriculum for pastors who serve in remote corners of the world where seminaries and Bible colleges are otherwise unavailable.

JAMES M. HAMILTON JR., Ph.D. is professor of Biblical Theology at The Southern Baptist Theological Seminary, and Senior Pastor of Kenwood Baptist Church, both in Louisville, KY. Dr. Hamilton is part of the BibleTalk podcast team with Dr. Sam Emadi and Alex Duke, and Hamilton is the author of *Typology—Understanding the Bible's Promise Shaped Patterns,* a two-volume commentary on *Psalms,* and several books on biblical theology, including *What Is Biblical Theology?* and *God's Glory in Salvation through Judgment: A Biblical Theology.*

DAVID S. KOTTER, Ph.D., is the Dean of the School of Theology and Professor of New Testament Studies at Colorado Christian University. Dr. Kotter was the co-founder and served as the Research Director of the Faith and Work Project at The Southern Baptist Theological Seminary. He has contributed to several books, including *The Bible and Money: Issues of Economy and Socioeconomic Ethics in the Bible* (Sheffield-Phoenix Press, 2020) and *For the Least of These: A Biblical Answer to Poverty* (Zondervan, 2015).

MICHAEL P. NAYLOR, Ph.D., is associate professor of Bible at Columbia International University in Columbia, South Carolina. He is the NT book review editor for the *Journal of the Evangelical Theological Society* and is the author of *Complexity and Creativity: John's Presentation of Jesus in the Book of Revelation* (Gorgias Press, 2018).

ROBERT L. PLUMMER, Ph.D., is the Collin and Evelyn Aikman Professor of Biblical Studies at The Southern Baptist Theological Seminary, Louisville, KY. Dr. Plummer is the host of the popular Daily Dose of Greek screencast and author, editor, or co-author of several books, including *40 Questions About Interpreting the Bible* (Kregel, 2010, 2021), *Beginning with New Testament Greek* (B&H Academic, 2020), and *Going Deeper with New Testament Greek* (B&H Academic, 2016, 2020).

MICHAEL E. POHLMAN, Ph.D., is Associate Professor of Christian Preaching and Pastoral Ministry at The Southern Baptist Theological Seminary, Louisville, KY. Dr. Pohlman is the author of *Broadcasting the Faith: Protestant Religious Radio and Theology in America, 1920 – 1950* (Wipf & Stock, 2021) and co-host (with Dr. Michael Haykin) of Bede: History for the Church, a weekly podcast on church history.

TODD A. SCACEWATER, Ph.D., is Assistant Professor in the College of International Studies at Dallas International University, Dallas, TX. He is the author of *The Divine Builder in Psalm 68: Jewish and Pauline Tradition* (T&T Clark, 2020) and editor of *Discourse Analysis of the New Testament Writings* (Fontes, 2020).

ABENEAZER G. URGA, Ph.D., is a professor in Biblical Studies at the Evangelical Theological College in Addis Ababa, Ethiopia, and he is an adjunct professor at Columbia International University. He is a member of Equip International and SIL Ethiopia. He has authored several books and articles. His forthcoming books include *Intercession of Jesus in Hebrews*.

MATTHEW D. WESTERHOLM, Ph.D., serves as Associate Professor of Church Music and Worship at the Southern Baptist Theological Seminary in Louisville, KY. He has written congregational songs and articles on worship for the websites of Desiring God, Gospel Coalition, and Doxology & Theology. Matthew is comfortable behind a piano but only feels at home with his wife, Lisa, and their three sons.

Preface

ONE OF THE CONTRIBUTORS to this book, Ben Cornish, provides theological training in the most unreached places of the world.[1] He often spends a week or two in "the middle of nowhere" as he teaches pastors the fundamentals of the Christian faith. Ben avers that one of the most pressing theological needs around the world is countering the false teaching of the "prosperity gospel." Even if you are reading this book from your recliner in Atlanta, Georgia, you have certainly encountered such teaching yourself—probably even on primetime TV! Prosperity gospel teachers claim that God wants his people to be healthy and wealthy, and if a person is not rich and well, it is because of that person's lack of faith.[2] This distortion of the Bible's teaching needs to be answered faithfully and winsomely. You will find such responses in the chapters of this volume.

Before diving into the volume, I encourage you to take a few moments to read through the brief biographical notes on the contributors (in alphabetical order of last name) on page xii. The chapters of the book, however, are not in alphabetical order of author. The chapter order reflects a more logical development of the topic, as you can see through the list of brief descriptions below. *Tolle Lege!* (Take up and read!)

- Chapter 1: Ben Cornish cogently argues that some of the distinctive doctrines of the prosperity gospel had their origin in

---

[1] See the ministry which he leads: teachingtruthinternational.org.

[2] Wording adapted from Robert L. Plummer, *40 Questions About Interpreting the Bible*, 2nd ed. (Grand Rapids: Kregel, 2021), 331.

a syncretism of metaphysical religious sects and Christianity. In other words, the prosperity gospel was tainted from the beginning, receiving its core tenets from outside the orthodox faith.

- Chapter 2: James Hamilton guides the reader on a biblical-theological journey through Proverbs and Ecclesiastes, showing how these books' teachings on wealth and poverty cohere within the unfolding story of the Bible.

- Chapter 3: Michael Pohlman challenges the reader to consider Paul's theology of suffering and what embracing that theology means not only for ministry but for a seminary's curriculum.

- Chapter 4: David Kotter delights the reader with a statistical journey, demonstrating the changing contours of wealth and poverty throughout history. Kotter shows how these economic patterns have resulted in evolving spiritual temptations for persons of all financial means.

- Chapter 5: Michael Naylor serves as our hermeneutical instructor, teaching us how the "glittering streets of gold" in the Apocalypse of John (and similar descriptions of opulence in the book) should not be misused to glorify riches or encourage God's people to pursue them.

- Chapter 6: Matthew Westerholm challenges churches to be wise in their selection of worship songs. Can churches sing songs written by prosperity gospel leaders?

- Chapter 7: Ethiopian scholar Abeneazer Urga assesses why the prosperity gospel has taken hold in Africa and employs Hebrews 13:1–6 to critique it.

- Chapter 8: Todd Scacewater helps the reader understand how the Greco-Roman culture surrounding early Christian communities would have understood "blessing, "happiness," or "the good life." In establishing the cultural and linguistic setting for these ideas, Scacewater enables us to hear the New Testament's teaching more clearly.

- Chapter 9: Indonesian scholar Philip Chia offers a detailed and technical assessment of what "prosperity" entails in Genesis chapter 39. The story of Joseph prospering during suffering is instructive for us today.

Robert L. Plummer

1

An Evaluation of the Historical Apologetic against "Word-Faith Theology"

Benjamin T. Cornish

IN 1982, DANIEL R. MCCONNELL developed an historical apologetic against the "prosperity gospel," also known as Word-Faith theology. After submitting his argument as a master's thesis, he later published it in the book *A Different Gospel*.[1] Using side-by-side textual comparisons, McConnell demonstrated that Kenneth Hagin (1917–2003) was not the true father of the modern expression of prosperity preaching, for he had plagiarized all of his distinctive doctrines from Essek William Kenyon (1867–1948), a man who ministered a generation before.[2] McConnell then accused Kenyon of developing his theology by syncretizing Christian doctrine with the philosophies of metaphysical religious sects, such as New Thought and Christian Science.[3] The intention of this argument was to show that from its inception, the prosperity gospel was not entirely Christian, thus adding an historical component to the previously used apologetic arguments based in biblical exegesis and theological analysis. For forty years now, scholars have debated whether Kenyon was, in fact, guilty of syncretism.[4] In this essay, I will argue that McConnell's disputed

---

1 Daniel R. McConnell, "The Kenyon Connection: A Theological and Historical Analysis of the Cultic Origins of the Faith Movement" (Master's thesis, Oral Roberts University, 1982); idem, *A Different Gospel*, updated ed. (Hendrickson, 1995). In some respects, McConnell was following the lead of his mentor, Charles Farah, who had penned one of the first scholarly protests against the opulence in Word-Faith circles. Charles Farah, *From the Pinnacle of the Temple: Faith vs. Presumption* (Logos International, 1979).

2 For this textual comparison, see McConnell, *A Different Gospel*, 8–11.

3 McConnell, *A Different Gospel*, 92.

4 Several authors followed in support of McConnell's argument, such as

claim is valid: Kenyon's distinctive Word-Faith doctrines represent a syncretistic blend of metaphysical thought and evangelical Christianity. To support my thesis, I will first introduce the core teachings of New Thought and then outline the arguments of the two primary sides of the debate. After evaluating the strengths and weaknesses of these arguments, I will defend McConnell's primary contention with additional historical evidence that neither author had thoroughly investigated.

Introducing New Thought

New Thought is a religious philosophy that incorporates aspects of numerous worldviews, including distorted versions of George Berkeley's idealism, Eastern religions, and Christianity, to name a few. Scholars of American new religious movements, like Catherine Albanese and Charles Braden, classify New Thought as a "metaphysical" sect or religion.[5] Not to be confused with the study of ontology, metaphysical religions were religious groups that developed in reaction to Baconianism—that is, the perception of science as the unique path to reliable knowledge.[6] The metaphysical religions opposed this empiricism, fiercely distrusting any knowledge learned through the senses.[7]

Terris H. Neuman, "Cultic Origins of World-Faith Theology within the Charismatic Movement," *Pneuma* 12, no. 1 (1990): 32–55; Hank Hanegraaff, *Christianity in Crisis* (Harvest House, 1993); Dave Hunt and T. A. McMahon, *The Seduction of Christianity: Spiritual Discernment in the Last Days* (Harvest House, 1987). The first major rebuttal of McConnell's argument was in William DeArteaga, *Quenching the Spirit: Discover the REAL Spirit behind the Charismatic Controversy*, 2nd ed. (Charisma House, 1996). Arguably the most impressive, though not the last, critique of McConnell's argument was in Robert M. Bowman Jr., *The Word-Faith Controversy: Understanding the Health and Wealth Gospel* (Baker Books, 2001).

5 See Catherine Albanese, *A Republic of Mind and Spirit: A Cultural History of American Metaphysical Religion* (Yale University Press, 2007); Charles Braden, *Spirits in Rebellion: The Rise and Development of New Thought: The Story of the Beginnings and Growth of New Thought and Kindred American Metaphysical Healing Movements*, 2nd ed. (Southern Methodist University Press, 1987).

6 See Catherine Albanese's article "Introduction: Awash in a Sea of Metaphysics," *JAAR* 75, no. 3 (September 2007): 582–585.

7 The irony of this distrust is the presentation of their worldviews as scientific.

Most scholars of New Thought attribute its origin to Phineas Quimby (1802–1866), but far more influential in New England was New Thought author Warren Felt Evans (1817–1889), who propagated his worldview through publication.[8] Between 1869 and 1884, Evans wrote seven books in which he articulated and defended New Thought. To understand this worldview, one must begin with its five foundational principles. First, New Thought is based in ontological idealism, which means that the material world is an emanation of the spiritual world, making it a lesser form of the same substance. Yet for New Thought, the material world is also less real than the spiritual.[9] Evans's ontology affected his view of Supreme Reality. The second principle therefore states that God is not the personal triune God of Christianity but is more like "the One" as perceived by monistic religions like Buddhism.[10] Third, humans are divine. Evans explained that the infinite One created millions of finite versions of himself—the souls of men and women. Evans was also adamant that humans are not their bodies.[11]

One can see this in the name "Christian Science." They believed that *true* science, however, was the study of the mind and spirit.

8 Catherine Albanese is one of the leading scholars on New Thought today. For a deep study of the origin and spread of metaphysical religions in American history, including New Thought, see Albanese, *A Republic of Mind and Spirit*. See also Warren Felt Evans and Catherine Albanese, *The Spiritual Journals of Warren Felt Evans: From Methodism to Mind Cure* (Indiana University Press, 2016).

9 Evans stated that "the animal soul of man is an individualized expression of [matter]." See Warren Felt Evans, *The Primitive Mind-Cure, The Nature and Power of Faith; Or, Elementary Lessons in Christian Philosophy and Transcendental Medicine* (H. H. Carter & Karrick, 1884), 143.

10 In Evans's view, "God is the only reality," and "this necessary being comprises all reality." See Warren Felt Evans, *The Divine Law of Cure* (H. H. Carter & Karrick, 1884), 32. Upon critique from his contemporaries, Evans would backpedal from his monism, suggesting that "it is not necessary to deny the personality of God as some have done." Despite this claim, Evans defined the "personality" of his god as a divine personification of "Love and Wisdom," and all of his prior books had described the divine one in monistic terms. See idem, *Esoteric Christianity and Mental Therapeutics* (H. H. Carter & Karrick, 1886), 154–155.

11 According to Evans, "the spirit of man is a finite limitation of the Universal Spirit, the Christ of Paul, and the true light of every man that cometh into the world." See Evans, *The Primitive Mind-Cure*, 78. Evans belittles deductive reasoning as well, except when it accords with one's intuition. See idem, *The Primitive Mind-Cure*, 49; idem, *The Divine Law of Cure*, 14.

Belief in these three principles produced the fourth, which is the law of attraction. This law described the supposed attractive or magnetic force that pulsed through the universe, enabling the human mind to change the physical world through the power of belief. If like attracts like, then positive thoughts in the mental realm would attract positive realities in the material realm. The law of attraction implied that a person could heal his or her body of disease. For New Thought believers, however, the mind was not only the savior from physical maladies but also the cause of them: negative thinking would attract negative realities. Fifth and finally, New Thought authors justified their worldview by appealing to an epistemology of intuition. In Evans's mind, the material world was inherently deceptive, and knowledge discovered by the senses was misleading. If the human mind was divine, however, then true knowledge would be attainable through intuition.[12] Evans described proper intuition as "the reality of a present inspiration from God," which should lead one to true and complete knowledge of him.[13] If this intuition was basic to human nature, then one could expect to find these principles in all of the religions and philosophies through history. This explains why, throughout his books, Evans appealed to the Alchemists of the Hermetic tradition, the Jewish mystics of the Kabala, the Vedic scriptures of Hinduism, and numerous Western philosophers. He also frequently quoted from the New Testament as though Jesus, John, and Paul had discovered New Thought two thousand years ago.[14]

From this short introduction, one should recognize that New Thought is thoroughly non-Christian. If Kenyon did syncretize New Thought with Christianity, then McConnell was right to be concerned, and apologists should utilize this historical apologetic, tracing Word-Faith theology back to this non-Christian metaphysical influence.

---

    12 Evans frequently attacked the trustworthiness of the senses. For numerous examples, see his chapter titled "Disease Exists Only in the Mind on the Plane of Sense, Which Is the Region of Deceptive Appearances" in *The Primitive Mind-Cure* (pp. 55–62).

    13 Evans, *The Divine Law of Cure*, 22.

    14 Evans, *The Primitive Mind-Cure*, 123.

McConnell's "Kenyon Connection"

McConnell defended his argument first by appealing to eyewitness testimony and circumstantial evidence to demonstrate that the metaphysical religions had influenced Kenyon's thinking. McConnell then performed a doctrinal comparison to show that Kenyon's theology was strikingly similar to the metaphysical religions.

McConnell's Evidence of Influence

Five years after McConnell published his master's thesis, Bruce Barron argued that Kenyon's roots went back to early Pentecostalism.[15] McConnell acknowledged this viewpoint in his book but dismissed it for several reasons, the most significant being that Kenyon had taught all of the distinctive Word-Faith doctrines, whereas his Pentecostal contemporaries had taught none of them. Further, even though Kenyon partnered in ministry with Pentecostals later in his life, he never embraced their two defining doctrines of Spirit-baptism as a work subsequent to conversion and glossolalia as the evidence of the baptism of the Holy Spirit.[16]

Putting Barron's theory behind him, McConnell introduced three types of historical evidence needed to validate his position. The best form of evidence would be a signed confession in which Kenyon admitted to some kind of influence from the metaphysical religions—but no such documents exist. The next best form of evidence would be eyewitness testimony. On this point, McConnell put forward two witnesses. First, John Kennington had claimed that Kenyon had admitted to him that he had been influenced by Christian Science and that he affirmed some of its beliefs: "We discussed this similarity at that time. And he acknowledged the similarity . . . , saying, 'All that Christian Science lacks is the blood of Jesus Christ.'"[17] The second eyewitness was Ern Baxter, who could

---

15 Bruce Barron, *The Health and Wealth Gospel: What's Going on Today in a Movement That Has Shaped the Faith of Millions* (InterVarsity Press, 1987).

16 For McConnell's interaction with Barron, see McConnell, *A Different Gospel*, 21–24.

17 John Kennington, "E. W. Kenyon and the Metaphysics of Christian

remember hearing Kenyon speak favorably about several of Mary Baker Eddy's doctrines and believed that Eddy had "undoubtedly" influenced Kenyon's theology.[18] Eddy had been a practitioner of New Thought under the guidance of Phineas Quimby, New Thought's founder, until she decided to modify and formalize his teachings into a religious group, later named Christian Science.[19]

McConnell's third type of evidence was circumstantial, which his critics would later point out is never sufficient to prove a theory of influence. However, in the realm of apologetics, circumstantial evidence has its place, as it demonstrates probability.[20] One should not find fault in choosing a theory that best explains all of the relevant evidence simply because that evidence happens to be circumstantial. On this point, McConnell presented Kenyon's biography, noting Kenyon's exposure to many worldviews and his participation in the Unitarian Church.[21] Following a line of reasoning from New Thought expert Charles Braden, McConnell suggested that Kenyon had walked the "well-traveled path from Unitarianism to Transcendentalism to New Thought."[22] In 1892, Kenyon found himself surrounded by metaphysical teaching when he enrolled in the Emerson College of Oratory, which, according to McConnell, was a center of New Thought indoctrination.[23] Indeed, from this point forward, Kenyon's theology became increasingly aligned with New Thought, leading McConnell to conclude that from his short time at Emerson, Kenyon had developed a new hermeneutic through which to interpret the Bible.

McConnell's Doctrinal Comparison

After evaluating Kenyon's history, McConnell began to compare

---

Science" (unpublished written statement, 1986), cited in McConnell, *A Different Gospel*, 25.

    18 Ern Baxter, taped correspondence with McConnell, printed in McConnell, *A Different Gospel*, 25.

    19 For Eddy's historical background, see Braden, *Spirits in Rebellion*, 18–25.

    20 McConnell, *A Different Gospel*, 25.

    21 McConnell, *A Different Gospel*, 33.

    22 See Braden, *Spirits in Rebellion*, 27–30, quoted in McConnell, *A Different Gospel*, 33–34.

    23 McConnell, *A Different Gospel*, 35–37.

doctrines. He designed this section to show that all of Kenyon's Word-Faith teachings were closer to New Thought or Christian Science ideas than to parallel concepts in Christian theology. Kenyon's teachings included revelation knowledge, identification, the law of faith, healing exclusively through spiritual means, and prosperity as a divine right. Concerning *revelation knowledge*, McConnell argued that just like New Thought, Kenyon promoted the view that the immaterial world was greater than the material one and that perfect knowledge of God was attainable in this life.[24] The second doctrine for analysis was *identification*. Unlike the Keswick movement, in which the doctrine was first emphasized, Kenyon infused identification with unbiblical meaning, denying the physical nature of Christ's atonement.[25] He then proceeded to argue that Christ took upon himself a demonic nature so that he could enter hell, defeat Satan, and be born again. Therefore, when new believers identify with Christ, Kenyon argued, they exchange their own satanic natures for divine ones.[26] New Thought writers say little to nothing about the nature of Christ after his death, but McConnell was right in pointing out that they denied the physical element of the atonement and explicitly promoted a divinized view of humankind.

The third doctrine for comparison was the *law of faith*, which appeared to be nearly synonymous with New Thought's law of attraction. Kenyon had repeatedly translated Mark 11:22 as "have the faith *of* God,"[27] using this text as proof that God created the

---

[24] For Kenyon's explanation of revelation knowledge, see E. W. Kenyon, *Two Kinds of Knowledge* (Kenyon's Gospel Publishing Society, 1966). For McConnell's epistemological comparison, see McConnell, *A Different Gospel*, 103–106. McConnell quoted Quimby as recorded in Horatio Dresser, *The Quimby Manuscripts* (Citadel, 1980), 177.

[25] McConnell, *A Different Gospel*, 114.

[26] Kenyon wrote two books on this subject: E. W. Kenyon, *What Happened from the Cross to the Throne*, 12th ed. (Kenyon's Gospel Publishing Society, 1969); idem, *Identification: A Romance in Redemption* (Kenyon's Gospel Publishing Society, 1968).

[27] Kenyon, *The Two Kinds of Faith*, 103, quoted in McConnell, *A Different Gospel*, 139. Kenyon also wrote, "Jesus is the author and finisher of faith, and when we become New Creations we receive a measure of God's Faith (Rom. 12:3)." Idem, *New Creation Realities* (Kenyon's Gospel Publishing Society, 1945), 68.

universe through faith rather than through his omnipotence and will. The notion that God has faith would imply the existence of a powerful object outside of God in which he might put his faith.[28] This object of God's faith—some kind of cosmic law—sounded to McConnell like New Thought's view of the divine as an impersonal infinite force.

The fourth doctrine for review was Kenyon's belief that *sickness and healing were always spiritual in origin*. Kenyon argued in several of his books that the sick must convince themselves that their physical symptoms were false and instead say with faith, "I am healed."[29] This approach to healing is nearly identical to the healing methods of both New Thought and Christian Science. When one believes that one's body is healed, that belief allegedly generates such a reality. The only apparent difference between Kenyon and the metaphysical religions was that Kenyon believed that Jesus had made this healing possible, whereas Evans and Eddy believed that Jesus had been the example of what was already possible for all people.

Finally, McConnell addressed the doctrine of *prosperity*, but Kenyon is conspicuously missing from this section of the book. Instead, McConnell compared New Thought's law of prosperity with that of Kenneth Hagin, Kenneth Copeland, and Frederick Price.[30] Apparently, Kenyon had warned against greed, but he had also asserted the "abnormality for believers to be in bondage to poverty."[31] Despite the lack of strength in McConnell's fifth doctrinal comparison, his "Kenyon Connection" argument is undeniably weighty,

---

28 McConnell quoted Kenyon as saying that "faith-filled words brought the universe into being, and faith-filled words are ruling that universe today." Kenyon, *The Two Kinds of Faith*, 20, quoted in McConnell, *A Different Gospel*, 133.

29 For Kenyon's doctrine of healing, see E. W. Kenyon, *Jesus the Healer* (Kenyon's Gospel Publishing Society, 1940); idem, *The Hidden Man*, 5th ed. (Kenyon's Gospel Publishing Society, 1970).

30 In Kenyon's rejection of greed, he defined prosperity as "the ability to use the ability of God to help humanity." E. W. Kenyon, *Advanced Bible Course: Studies in the Deeper Life* (Kenyon's Gospel Publishing Society, 1970), 59, quoted in McConnell, *A Different Gospel*, 173.

31 Kenyon, *Jesus the Healer*, 67, quoted in McConnell, *A Different Gospel*, 173.

which explains why so many authors have reiterated his conclusion over the past four decades.

Robert Bowman's Response to McConnell

Soon after McConnell published his thesis, criticism followed. Arguably the most formidable critique came from theologian and apologist Robert Bowman Jr. in his 2001 book, *The Word-Faith Controversy*. Being opposed to the prosperity gospel, Bowman dedicated much of his book to critiquing Word-Faith theology; however, in his section on Word-Faith history, he took issue with McConnell's book. Bowman began by critiquing McConnell's methodology. He then challenged McConnell's position that Kenyon's doctrines were *essentially* metaphysical in nature. One will not find the words "essentially metaphysical" in McConnell's thesis statement, but McConnell did make similar assertions throughout his book, including the use of the word "cultic" in reference to the roots of Word-Faith theology.[32] Finally, Bowman tried to show that the most likely influence behind Kenyon's theology was the healing movements that preceded the birth of Pentecostalism.

McConnell's "Inadequate" Methodology

Bowman protested McConnell's methodology of comparing just a few of Kenyon's doctrines with those of New Thought, which would cause readers to assume that the two worldviews were nearly identical. A better methodology would be to compare Kenyon's theology to *all* of the doctrines of New Thought—twenty-three of them on Bowman's count. Bowman therefore created a diagram of three columns to compare the doctrines of New Thought with Christian Science and E.W. Kenyon. Based on this visual, Christian Science shared fifteen of the twenty-three doctrines of New Thought, while Kenyon shared only three.[33]

If McConnell's point had been that Kenyon had snuck *all* of

---

32 McConnell makes such comments from his introduction to conclusion in McConnell, *A Different Gospel*, xx–xxi, 185–186.
33 Bowman, *The Word-Faith Controversy*, 46–47.

New Thought into the church, then Bowman's critique would be valid, but this was not McConnell's aim. McConnell had argued that Kenyon had syncretized his *distinctive* Word-Faith doctrines from the metaphysical groups.[34] Bowman, however, would later strengthen his position by showing that Kenyon differed from metaphysical religion on the essential matters of their worldviews.[35] He also contended that Kenyon's distinctive Word-Faith doctrines were being taught by his contemporaries in the Holiness and Faith-Cure movements. These two factors gave Bowman probable grounds to dismiss the idea that Word-Faith theology is metaphysical in nature.

Kenyon's Five "Evangelical" Doctrines

In order to demonstrate the first premise above, Bowman showed how each of Kenyon's five allegedly metaphysical doctrines were actually different from New Thought and Christian Science. Concerning the doctrine of *revelation knowledge*, for example, Kenyon had argued that two types of knowledge exist—revelation knowledge and sense knowledge. The former, Kenyon argued, came from the Holy Spirit and was trustworthy, while the latter came from the senses and was not as trustworthy. McConnell had compared this view to the metaphysical religions' epistemologies that rejected sense knowledge in favor of intuition. Bowman responded by demonstrating that Kenyon had believed that the material world was dependent on the immaterial world but was still real; for Christian Science, however, the material world was illusory. As a result, Christian Scientists put no trust in sense knowledge, whereas Kenyon simply trusted it less than revelation knowledge.[36] Bowman proceeded to demonstrate how the next two of Kenyon's

---

34 McConnell stated openly that "much of the Faith theology is either evangelical or Pentecostal, but at key points its cultic origins are readily apparent." McConnell, *A Different Gospel*, 101. These key points are the focus of McConnell's thesis.

35 Bowman, *The Word-Faith Controversy*, 47; emphasis original.

36 Bowman, *The Word-Faith Controversy*, 48–49. In describing her epistemology, Eddy rewrote Luke 4:18 to say that Jesus came "to preach deliverance to the captives of sense," and she later contrasted spiritual knowledge with "sinful

doctrines differed from their counterparts in the metaphysical religions. Bowman agreed with McConnell, however, on his assessment of the fourth doctrine. To suggest that *sickness and healing are always spiritual in origin* and only manifest corporeally in the body is nearly identical to the New Thought doctrine that all sickness is caused in the spirit realm. Finally, concerning the doctrine of *prosperity*, Bowman correctly noted that McConnell had drawn no significant parallels between Kenyon and New Thought.[37]

After his assessment, Bowman unexpectedly affirmed that McConnell had discovered real similarities between New Thought and Kenyon, thereby demonstrating reasonable grounds to conclude that Kenyon had been influenced by these groups. Nevertheless, Bowman critiqued McConnell for failing to substantiate his more extreme comments that Kenyon's theology was *essentially* metaphysical in nature. Finally, Bowman argued that Kenyon should be identified as an evangelical who was theologically closest to the Faith-Cure movement.[38]

Bowman's "Kenyon Connection"

Bowman conceded that Kenyon had been influenced by those around him; thus, a "Kenyon connection" of some type did, in fact, exist. The connection, however, was not *primarily* to New Thought but to the Faith-Cure movement. Defining the Faith-Cure movement has proven difficult as it was not a denomination, creed, or monolithic association of churches. Joseph Williams has suggested that the key similarity among its advocates was the rejection of the exhortation to rejoice in suffering and the corresponding promotion of the view that God has already provided a guarantee of deliverance for every believer.[39]

---

sense." Mary Baker Eddy, *Science and Health with Key to the Scriptures* (Trustees, 1934), xi, 23.

37 Today, New Thought and Word-Faith teachers alike depict wealth as a "divine right" accessible through positive confession and cosmic law. See Bowman, *The Word-Faith Controversy*, 53.

38 Bowman, *The Word-Faith Controversy*, 54, 67.

39 Joseph W. Williams, *Spirit Cure: A History of Pentecostal Healing* (Oxford University Press, 2013), 3.

To support the claim that Kenyon was most comparable to these Faith-Cure evangelicals, Bowman first showed that Kenyon held to many core doctrines, like the infallibility of the Bible, the incarnation of Christ, the virgin birth, the physical substitutionary atonement of Christ, his future glorious return, and salvation by grace through faith alone.[40] For Bowman, Kenyon may have found an affinity with the Keswick branch of the Holiness movement that had interpreted faith as the ability to perceive of God's promises as present possessions. Bowman then revealed that eight of Kenyon's doctrines had predecessors in the healing movement. Most frequently cited in this section was A. B. Simpson, the founder of the Christian and Missionary Alliance.[41] Simpson had translated Mark 11:22 as "the faith *of* God" as early as 1915 and may have been the influence behind Kenyon's matching translation.[42] In reference to the *law of faith*, Bowman cited Hannah Whitall Smith, a leader in the Higher Life tradition who had taught a version of the law of faith that was nearly identical to that of Kenyon.[43] Moving through the list of Kenyon's doctrines, Bowman found evangelical predecessors for each one, such as John Lake's anthropology, Simpson's doctrine of the divine right of healing, and the Keswick teachers' confession of the fullness of the Spirit regardless of one's

---

40 Bowman, *The Word-Faith Controversy*, 67.

41 Bowman also gave John G. Lake significant attention, further proving that other evangelicals were teaching things similar to Kenyon's teaching. In the case of Lake, his theology was at times more aligned to metaphysical religion than was Kenyon's, especially his view of man: "Man is not a separate creation detached from God, he is part of God Himself.... God intends us to be gods." John G. Lake, *Spiritual Hunger, the God-Men and Other Sermons by John G. Lake*, ed. Gordon Lindsay (Christ for the Nations, 1976), 20–21.

42 Simpson believed that faith was the opposite of hope, for hope waits, while faith takes. A. B. Simpson, *The Lord for the Body*, rev. ed. (Christian, 1959), 123, quoted in Bowman, *The Word-Faith Controversy*, 70; idem, *The Gospel of Healing* (Christian, 1915), 142–143, quoted in Bowman, *The Word-Faith Controversy*, 70.

43 Hannah Whitall Smith, *The Christian's Secret of a Happy Life* (Fleming H. Revell, 1883), 195–96, cited in Bowman, *The Word-Faith Controversy*, 72. Bowman cites this reference as recorded in Dale H. Simmons, *E. W. Kenyon and the Postbellum Pursuit of Peace, Power, and Plenty*, Studies in Evangelicalism 13 (Scarecrow Press, 1996), 152.

sensory awareness.⁴⁴

In addition to the doctrinal similarities, Kenyon also shared the apologetic approach of some of those in the faith-healing ministries who perceived their theology as a corrective to the mental-healing practices of the metaphysicians. Charles Fox Parham, for example, conceded that Christian Scientists had at times accessed real power, but they had done so by "counterfeit" measures.⁴⁵ Kenyon likewise acknowledged similarities between his teaching and that of the metaphysicians, but he also stated openly that his teaching served as the correct version of the healing power they sought.⁴⁶ For Bowman, this explicit rejection of certain metaphysical doctrines was a compelling reason to reject McConnell's belief that Kenyon was more like the metaphysical groups than other Christians. In McConnell's mind, it was through Kenyon's apologetic technique that he ended up conceding some of the Mind-Cure principles in his attempt to correct others.⁴⁷

In summary, in responding to McConnell, Bowman was not attempting to prove that Kenyon was a Holiness teacher or that he was entirely *un*influenced by metaphysical religion. Instead, he demonstrated that Kenyon was relatively more akin to certain evangelicals than to metaphysical teachers. Bowman then posited his most important hypothesis: "The possibility exists that the evangelical Faith-Cure movement and early Pentecostalism were also influenced in some respects by metaphysical thought."⁴⁸ Unfortunately, in light of the complexity of substantiating this hypothesis, Bowman did not pursue the thought any further.

---

44 Bowman, *The Word-Faith Controversy*, 69–78.

45 Charles Fox Parham, *Kol Kare Bomidbar: A Voice Crying in the Wilderness* (Joplin, 1944), 26, quoted in Bowman, *The Word-Faith Controversy*, 80.

46 For example, Kenyon agreed with Mary Baker Eddy that sickness was not physical in origin and that healing would also not be physical in origin. She was wrong, however, for teaching that healing would be *mental* in nature rather than spiritual. See Kenyon, *Jesus the Healer*, 90.

47 McConnell devoted an entire chapter to prove that "in his attempt to help the church respond to the 'challenge' of the cults, Kenyon 'absorbed' metaphysical concepts in order to restore the healing ministry to the church." McConnell, *A Different Gospel*, 38.

48 Bowman, *The Word-Faith Controversy*, 82.

Evaluating the Original Arguments

McConnell and Bowman offered articulate arguments backed by significant research, and those interested in this subject will benefit from an examination of each of their works. Nevertheless, their arguments have weaknesses as well.

Evaluating McConnell's Argument

McConnell's argumentation has one primary weakness and one secondary weakness. First and foremost, McConnell failed to interact directly with the Holiness doctrines that resembled Kenyon's. McConnell could have set the doctrines side by side to show the differences, but he merely stated that they were unlike each other and footnoted Vinson Synan's book as a historical reference on the Holiness movement. Ironically, Synan would later align with McConnell's critics.[49] This failure on McConnell's part does not disprove his thesis, but it does allow for the possibility that someone else might later show that Kenyon's theology did reflect those of other evangelicals, just as Bowman did. Second, McConnell's accusations about Word-Faith theology's being "cultic" or "heretical" are not properly nuanced, and one might conclude from his book that Word-Faith churches have no born-again believers—a claim with which McConnell would not likely agree. Nevertheless, even if one argued that Kenyon's syncretism resulted in doctrines that were partially—rather than *essentially*—metaphysical, that statement would still support McConnell's primary contention that Kenyon committed syncretism. This second weakness is applicable, therefore, only to the tone of his book and not his thesis.

The strengths of McConnell's argument are threefold. First, as Bowman conceded, McConnell was correct in his contention that Kenyon's central Word-Faith doctrines resembled the teachings of metaphysicians. They were not identical, but McConnell's

---

49 Vinson Synan agreed with Joe McIntyre and Lewis Brogdon, both of whom were critical of McConnell's view of Kenyon. See Joe McIntyre, *E. W. Kenyon and His Message of Faith: The True Story*, 2nd ed. (Empowering Grace Ministries, 2010); Lewis Brogdon, *The New Pentecostal Message?* (Wipf & Stock, 2015).

accusation was syncretism, and syncretism always produces a *new* belief system that is not faithful to either of the originals. Second, McConnell's historical timeline may not conclusively prove *how* Kenyon's doctrines changed, but it does show *when* Kenyon first publicly taught different views from those of his childhood faith—namely, right after he studied at Emerson College. Third, McConnell's discovery of the two eyewitness testimonies demonstrates that Kenyon was not embarrassed by the similarities he shared with Christian Science. Based on these arguments, the best explanation for Kenyon's new doctrinal positions is that the teaching and culture of metaphysical religion at Emerson College must have affected his thinking to some degree.

Evaluating Bowman's Argument

Bowman's critique of McConnell's methodology has problems. If he really believed that his chart of doctrinal comparison was the best way to demonstrate overlap—or lack thereof—between worldviews, then one would expect him to provide this same type of chart when he attempted to prove the "greater" similarities between Kenyon's theology and the Faith-Cure movement. Instead, Bowman followed the same methodology as McConnell, highlighting just a sampling of doctrines that he saw as the most significant without demonstrating how much overall commonality Kenyon shared with the Holiness movement. What Bowman failed to note is that the number of similar doctrines between Kenyon and New Thought is a secondary issue. Far more important than the percentage shared is the centrality of those doctrines within Christian theology and whether the concepts truly originated from a non-Christian source.[50] Even if New Thought had affected only one of Kenyon's doctrines, if it led to a different gospel, then Scripture requires that elders warn Christians against that message (Gal 1:8–9; 1 Tim 1:3–4). McConnell has sounded the warning.

McConnell's first weakness was Bowman's strength; namely, Bowman successfully showed that Kenyon and some of his contemporary evangelicals had taught similar doctrines. Yet, Bowman

---

50 Bowman, *The Word-Faith Controversy*, 47.

was wrong to conclude that this phenomenon weakened McConnell's warning. It instead opened the door to a synthesis of viewpoints—the same synthesis about which Bowman had hypothesized. Is it possible that metaphysical religion had a wider influence on American Christianity than is normally acknowledged today? Below, I will argue in the affirmative: the best explanation of the historical evidence is that metaphysical religion had also influenced certain highly influential Faith-Cure evangelicals. If true, then Bowman's strongest critique of McConnell's thesis—his doctrinal comparison of Kenyon with evangelicals—becomes irrelevant, and McConnell's position remains the best explanation of events.

The Bedfellows of Faith-Cure and Metaphysics

The charge of common syncretism is best understood against the backdrop of a certain spiritual milieu in nineteenth-century America, particularly among those who were wary of hardnosed philosophical naturalism. Historian of American metaphysical religion, Catherine Albanese, has argued that church historians have devoted significant attention to only two of the three primary "religious forces at work in early America": mainline denominations and of evangelicalism.[51] Overlooked by most has been the influence of metaphysical religion. In her monumental work *A Republic of Mind and Spirit*, Albanese explained the cultural factors that prepared America for groups like New Thought, Transcendentalism, and Christian Science.[52] Spiritual curiosity had marked the religious landscape, particularly in the realm of mind-science, magic, and religious syncretism. With the newly minted American Constitution promising religious freedom, Americans exited the eighteenth century with a peculiar blend of thankfulness to God and confidence in the self. Lingering memories from the Age of Enlightenment affirmed that nothing was impossible for the human mind, an attitude further bolstered by the Industrial Revolution. Such optimism, combined with innovations in medicine, created

---

51 Albanese, "Introduction: Awash in a Sea of Metaphysics," 582.
52 Albanese, *A Republic of Mind and Spirit*, 21–118.

a breed of pseudo-scientists like Franz Anton Mesmer who sought to integrate science with spirituality. The notion that people could cure themselves by means of the mind became a longed-for gospel among those curious about innovative healing methods.[53]

Those who rejected philosophical naturalism hungered for a spirituality that promoted miracles for modernity.[54] Many found what they were looking for in the sermons of revivalist preachers like Charles Finney (1792–1875) and the crusades that followed from the late 1850s to the early 1900s, a period sometimes referred to as the Third Great Awakening.[55] Unlike the First Great Awakening, which had been marked by Reformed preaching, the Second and Third were more anti-intellectual in tone and tended to promote "decisions for Christ," perfectionism, and outward manifestations of the Spirit, like miraculous healing.[56] Thus, during the same decades when Quimby, Evans, and Eddy were establishing their mental-healing ministries, Finney and others, like D. L. Moody, were promoting concepts like "prevailing prayer." In a lecture series on revival, Finney stated that when a Christian has "faith in prayer," this faith "always does obtain the blessing sought."[57] His lectures gave credence to the notion that faith is a force—an idea that would mesh well with New Thought.

When reading about New Thought today, however, one may come to the false conclusion that it could not have been influential

---

53 With the migration of the occult from England, the traditional voodoo religions of Africa among slaves, and the presence of Native American shamanism, America was peppered with individuals engaged in mystical pagan philosophies and healing techniques. See Albanese, *A Republic of Mind and Spirit*, chaps. 1–2 (pp. 66–118, 180–182). On Mesmer and Mesmerism, see pp. 190–192.

54 For a discussion on the development of the Holiness movement concurrent with "Darwinism, higher criticism, [and] the social gospel," see Vinson Synan, *The Holiness-Pentecostal Tradition: Charismatic Movements in the Twentieth Century*, 2nd ed. (Eerdmans, 1997), 20, 31, 45–46. Apparently, both Holiness and Pentecostal teachers saw themselves as the correction to anti-supernaturalist trends.

55 Walter Hampel, "Prayer Revivals and the Third Great Awakening," *Evangelical Review of Theology* 31, no. 1 (January 2007): 30–42.

56 Michael Scott Horton, "The Legacy of Charles Finney," *Modern Reformation* 4, no. 1 (January 1995): 5–9.

57 Charles Finney, *Lectures on Revivals of Religion*, 2nd ed. (Leavitt, Lord & Co., 1835), 65.

among Christians since it rejected organized religion. Quimby certainly refused to formalize New Thought into a group of any kind, but for one to conclude that New Thought had no influence on the church would be a mistake. The writings of Evans clearly indicate that New Thought philosophers saw their worldview as the truest form of Christianity. Further, at some point during the nineteenth century, some New Thought philosophers began swapping lecterns with Faith-Cure preaching ministers who shared similar ideas about the central role of positive thinking in physical healing.

This trend can be found in Kenyon's day as some of his contemporary Faith-Cure preachers had close relationships with metaphysicians. The primary example worth considering here is the friendship of Charles Cullis and Charles Wesley Emerson. Cullis was one of the central leaders in the early Faith-Cure movement, and much of his influence came through Faith Training School, the institution he founded.[58] Emerson, in contrast, was a Unitarian minister in Massachusetts. In 1880, he founded the Emerson College of Oratory, where Kenyon would later study. Yet, between 1876 and 1887, "Emerson served ... on the faculty of Cullis's Faith Training College" and, according to Bowman, was "apparently comfortable theologically and practically with the movement represented by Cullis."[59] While teaching at Cullis's college, Emerson's worldview became increasingly aligned with metaphysics, even as he continued to teach evangelical students who would become the future Faith-Cure ministers.[60] The fact that Emerson was comfortable with Cullis' theology is less surprising than the inverse—that

---

58 Raymond Cunningham also notes that "Simpson was soon recognized as a leader of the faith cure school, second only to Charles Cullis." Raymond J. Cunningham, "From Holiness to Healing: The Faith Cure in America 1872–1892," *CH* 43, no. 4 (December 1974): 503 (pp. 499–513).

59 Bowman, *The Word-Faith Controversy*, 65. Benjamin Hartley has attested to this fact as well, though he would not likely affirm the thesis of this essay. See Benjamin Loren Hartley, *Evangelicals at a Crossroads: Revivalism and Social Reform in Boston, 1860–1910* (University of New Hampshire Press, 2011), 60.

60 John M. Coffee and Richard Lewis Wentworth, *A Century of Eloquence: The History of Emerson College, 1880–1980* (Alternative, 1982), 10. Judith Ann Matta also demonstrated the intimate relationship between Emerson and the Christian Science throughout her book. See Judith A. Matta, *The Born Again Jesus of the Word-Faith Teaching* (Spirit of Truth Ministry, 1987).

Cullis considered Emerson to be a faithful Christian minister. Even as late as 1885, five years after Emerson started his own school, Cullis continued to praise him: "Prof. C. W. Emerson . . . is one of the few elocutionists fit to be trusted to teach people how to speak in the name of the Lord."[61]

One marker of Charles Cullis's impact on the American church was his influence on A. B. Simpson and, by extension, the denomination that Simpson founded. One historian argued that Simpson's entire doctrine of healing owed its existence to Cullis.[62] If Cullis was the fountainhead of theological education for the Faith-Cure movement and was comfortable with his students' learning from Emerson, then one can see how they might develop theologies biased toward metaphysical religion and why their doctrines resembled those of Kenyon.[63]

More research must be done on this subject; nevertheless, sufficient evidence exists to indicate some level of syncretistic relationships between metaphysicians and Faith-Cure preachers.[64]

---

61 Charles Cullis, quoted in William H. Daniels, *Dr. Cullis and His Work* (Garland, 1885), 362.

62 Charles Nienkirchen, *A. B. Simpson and the Pentecostal Movement* (Hendrickson, 1992), 14.

63 One way of rebutting McConnell's thesis is to reject that Emerson College promoted New Thought, but the evidence suggests otherwise. Ralph Waldo Trine, one of the most famous New Thought philosophers, first embraced New Thought while studying at Emerson in 1891. Joe McIntyre has shown that this was the very same year that Kenyon attended. The timeline supports the notion that the culture at Emerson was to propagate a metaphysical interpretation of the Bible. See McIntyre, *Kenyon and His Message of Faith*, 18–19. McIntyre, however, would disagree with this essay. For a summary of his view, see the appendix below.

64 A second example is the partnership of Henry Drummond and D. L. Moody. Drummond spoke as a guest teacher at Emerson College and wrote metaphysical theology, but he also preached alongside popular evangelicals. He was also a close friend of Moody. Those who would claim that Drummond was not a metaphysician should read Horatio Dresser's work. Dresser was a New Thought philosopher in the nineteenth-century who relied on Drummond's writings. See Horatio W. Dresser, ed., *The Journal of Practical Metaphysics: Devoted to the Unification of Scientific and Spiritual Thought and the New Philosophy of Health* 2, nos. 1–12 (October 1897): 1–359. Today, one finds Drummond listed as "an essential New Thought Author" in modern New Thought catalogues, such as New Thought Streams, "New Thought Library," last modified 2014, http://

The influence appears to have been mutual, and their doctrines so closely aligned that, at times, they felt comfortable having each other lecture in their respective schools.

Conclusion

McConnell accused Kenyon of syncretizing Christianity with metaphysical religion, and Kenyon's history and theology bear evidence of this accusation. Bowman believed that Kenyon was more aligned with the Faith-Cure movement, as depicted in the doctrines of evangelicals like A. B. Simpson and Charles Cullis.[65] This aspect of Bowman's thesis was correct, but he left his most important hypothesis unexplored. The synthesis of McConnell's and Bowman's distinct positions is that metaphysical thought had also influenced Faith-Cure leaders like Simpson and Cullis. Kenyon and these preachers had accused New Thought and Christian Science of seizing God's legitimate power through illegitimate means, but their critique did not go far enough. Instead of rejecting the teaching of Christian Science and New Thought outright and building their theology on Scripture, they affirmed certain metaphysical principles and then used those principles to interpret the Bible. McConnell's original thesis therefore remains the best explanation of events, and his warning valid: Christians should reject the false teaching of Word-Faith theology as a syncretistic blend of evangelical and metaphysical thought.

---

newthoughtstreams.com/authors.htm. The overlap in Drummond's ministry between New Thought and the faith-cure movement is troubling. For additional connections between metaphysics and faith-cure, see Bowman, *The Word Faith Controversy*, 81–82; Kevin Scott Smith, "Mind, Might, and Mastery: Human Potential in Metaphysical Religion and E. W. Kenyon" (Master's thesis, Liberty University, 1995).

65 Bowman, *The Word-Faith Controversy*, 81–82.

Appendix: More Recent Research on Word-Faith Origins

When Bowman published *The Word-Faith Controversy* in 2001, he was right to identify two apparent sides to the debate regarding the influences on E. W. Kenyon.[66] In the decades since, however, new publications have continued the conversation, including new positions and arguments not identical to the views outlined above. Below, I offer an annotated bibliography of some of these perspectives on the debate.[67] These works are meant to be *indicative* of more recent academic contributions, not *constitutive* of a comprehensive list.

John Haller and Kate Bowler: New Thought and Holiness Influence

In 2012, John S. Haller Jr. wrote *The History of New Thought: From Mind Cure to Positive Thinking and the Prosperity Gospel*. Writing as an historian of New Thought rather than as a Christian theologian, Haller makes an assessment worth noting. According to him, Kenyon was influenced by both New Thought and the early Pentecostal movement, which meant that his theology landed somewhere in between the two.[68] In 2013, Kate Bowler made a bigger news splash with her publication *Blessed: A History of the American Prosperity Gospel*. Bowler arrived at a conclusion similar to Haller's: Kenyon had been influenced by both movements.[69]

---

66 Bowman, *The Word-Faith Controversy*, 38–41.

67 Several important publications have been left out of this review of scholarship because they were included in Bowman's survey of publications in *The Word-Faith Controversy*, 7–11. Others were excluded because they offered little in the way of original argumentation, such as Hanegraaff's *Christianity in Crisis* or Andrew Perriman's *Faith, Health, and Prosperity: A Report on Word of Faith and Positive Confession Theologies* (Paternoster Press, 2003). Others have been excluded because their historical argumentation makes Kenyon's origins a non-issue.

68 See John S. Haller, *The History of New Thought: From Mind Cure to Positive Thinking and the Prosperity Gospel* (Swedenborg Foundation Press, 2012), 268–272.

69 Bowler explains that Kenyon "flatly rejected" New Thought because it

These two publications provide historical perspectives from opposite sides of the timeline: Haller began with New Thought and traced its influence forward, connecting it through Kenyon to the modern prosperity movement. Bowler, on the other hand, began with the prosperity gospel and traced its history back from Kenneth Hagin to Kenyon to New Thought.

Joe McIntyre: Holiness Influence

In 1997, Joe McIntyre published his book *E. W. Kenyon and His Message of Faith: The True Story*. This book preceded Bowman's, but I include it here because Bowman did not interact with it. In the book's second edition, McIntyre engaged more primary sources, including "unpublished articles, sermons, previously unknown periodicals from Kenyon's early days, some manuscripts, an old Bible, and some hymn books, a brief journal, many, many sermon notebooks, lots of poems, and other odds and ends."[70]

McIntyre exonerated Kenyon from the charge of syncretism with a defense resembling that of Bowman but without the ensuing critique of Word-Faith teaching. McIntyre defended his view with his perspective on Kenyon's time at Emerson, a doctrinal assessment, as well as a study of seven individuals from the Holiness and Keswick movements. These included Phoebe Palmer, Charles Cullis, Alexander Dowie, A. B. Simpson, Andrew Murray, D. L. Moody, and Kelso Carter.[71] These evangelicals, McIntyre believed, shaped Kenyon into the theologian he became. In my estimation, this second aspect of McIntyre's defense fits with my contention

---

substituted God's spiritual laws with "abstract principles." Nevertheless, Kenyon also "appropriated New Thought's focus on mind, spirit, and universal laws to show that Christians could look to the cross not as a promise of things to come, but as a guarantee of benefits *already* granted." Bowler also reveals significant evidence that Kenyon worked closely with the Keswick branch of the Holiness movement and adopted many of their doctrines. See Kate Bowler, *Blessed: A History of the American Prosperity Gospel* (New York: Oxford University Press, 2013), 15–17.

70 McIntyre, *E. W. Kenyon and His Message of Faith*, vii.

71 Much of McIntyre's treatment of the Holiness movement and various Faith-Cure influences are found in *E. W. Kenyon and His Message of Faith*, chaps. 6–10 (pp. 42–101).

that metaphysics had a wider influence on Christianity. Despite Dale Simmons's critique of McIntyre's book as embodying the "hagiographic extreme," the book is nevertheless an important read for anyone interested in the subject.[72]

Geir Lie: Dispensationalist Influence

In 1996, Geir Lie published "E. W. Kenyon: Cult Founder or Evangelical Minister?"[73] Lie followed this article with three more accounts of Kenyon: a second article in 2000, a book in 2003, and a third article in 2008.[74] Similar to Bowman, Lie's first three publications sought to demonstrate that Kenyon was primarily the product of the Higher Life and Holiness movements, but his 2008 article explored another influence—one that, to my knowledge, had not been detected by others. Lie suggested that "Kenyon was heavily influenced by dispensational beliefs during the first phase of his ministry" and "that the 'remnants' of dispensationalism" remained throughout Kenyon's publications, which may explain some of the inconsistencies in his theology.[75] Those interested in pursuing further research on Kenyon, especially for an opposing view to my own, should consult Lie's publications.

Kirk MacGregor: Cult Influence

Kirk MacGregor has taken the outlier position on the origins of

---

72 See Dale Simmons, review of *E. W. Kenyon: Cult Leader or Evangelical Minister?*, by Geir Lie, *Pneuma* 27, no. 1 (2005): 204–205. Simmons wrote his PhD dissertation on Kenyon and is now considered a Kenyon expert. In contrast to McIntyre's unapologetic defense of Kenyon, Simmons has indicated that Lie's favorable treatment of Kenyon (see below) is more even-handed.

73 Geir Lie, "E. W. Kenyon Cult Founder or Evangelical Minister?," *European Pentecostal Theological Association Bulletin* 16 (1996): 71–86.

74 Geir Lie, "The Theology of E. W. Kenyon: Plain Heresy or within the Boundaries of Pentecostal-Charismatic 'Orthodoxy'?," *Pneuma* 22, no. 1 (Spring 2000): 85–114; idem, *E. W. Kenyon, Cult Founder or Evangelical Minister? An Historical Analysis of Kenyon's Theology with Particular Emphasis on Roots and Influences* (Refleks, 2003); idem, "E. W. Kenyon and Dispensationalism," *Cyberjournal for Pentecostal-Charismatic Research* 17 (January 2008): 1–17.

75 Lie, "Kenyon and Dispensationalism," 2.

the Word-Faith movement, as seen in the name of his article: "The Word-Faith Movement: A Theological Conflation of the Nation of Islam and Mormonism?"[76] Without dismissing McConnell's "Kenyon Connection," MacGregor labeled that approach "monotraditional and sociological in character."[77] MacGregor noted that Kenyon's theological anthropology had no corollaries in either evangelicalism or New Thought. MacGregor then sought to prove that the Nation of Islam and Mormonism were the primary influences on the modern Word-Faith movement. For MacGregor, Kenyon could not have been the source of the divinized Word-Faith anthropology. MacGregor believed he could therefore disregard the doctrinal similarities between Kenyon's law of faith, the Faith-Cure movement's view of prayer, and New Thought's law of attraction.[78] MacGregor supported his claim by showing that Word-Faith preacher Frederick K. C. Price had extensive knowledge of the Nation of Islam and incorporated it into his own theology. Benny Hinn and Kenneth Copeland then "expanded and disseminated Price's teachings via their respective multimedia facilities."[79] In this way, while not dismissing the influence of Kenyon entirely, MacGregor proposed and defended his view that two new non-Christian religious movements influenced the Word-Faith doctrine of anthropology.

Paul King: Historical Precedent

The final work worthy of inclusion is one whose thesis I wholeheartedly reject, namely, Paul King's 2008 book *Only Believe: Examining the Origin and Development of Classic and Contemporary*

---

76 Kirk MacGregor, "The Word-Faith Movement: A Theological Conflation of the Nation of Islam and Mormonism?," *JAAR* 75 (2007): 87–120.
77 MacGregor, "The Word-Faith Movement," 89.
78 MacGregor, "The Word-Faith Movement," 91.
79 MacGregor, "The Word-Faith Movement," 104. Latter-Day Saints scholar Daniel Peterson has also noted this connection. According to Peterson, "Copeland's exegetical remarks could have been drawn from the wellsprings of 'only the Latter-day Saints, to whom a doctrine ... of human beings and of their literal kinship with God has been revealed.'" Daniel Peterson, *The Last Days: Teaching of the Modern Prophets* (Aspen Books, 1998), 71.

Word of Faith Theologies. Believing that Kenyon was irrelevant to Word-Faith history, King became the first—and, to my knowledge, only—author to attempt to find support for his doctrine from the Church Fathers. Conceding that no *direct* link exists, he attempted to show that the ideas within Word-Faith theology have historical precedent in the writings of Clement of Alexandria, Cyril of Jerusalem, Augustine, Leo the Great, Gregory the Great, and Anselm, among others.[80]

---

80 Paul L. King, *Only Believe: Examining the Origin and Development of Classic and Contemporary Word of Faith Theologies* (Word & Spirit Press, 2008), 25–27.

2

Wealth and Poverty in Proverbs and Ecclesiastes

James M. Hamilton Jr.

> *All the days of the afflicted are evil, but the cheerful of heart has a continual feast. Better is a little with the fear of the LORD than great treasure and trouble with it. Better is a dinner of herbs where love is than a fattened ox and hatred with it.*
> Proverbs 15:15–17[1]

Introduction: Social Justice, Wealth, and Solomon's Teaching

IN THE PROLOGUE to his National Book Award winning *Stamped from the Beginning*, Ibram X. Kendi writes,

> Federal data show that the median wealth of White households is a staggering *thirteen times* the median wealth of Black households .... If Black people make up 13.2 percent of the US population, then Black people should ... [be] somewhere close to owning 13 percent of US wealth. But today, the United States remains nowhere close to racial parity. African Americans own 2.7 percent of the nation's wealth.[2]

In the third edition of their popular introduction to *Critical Race Theory*, Richard Delgado and Jean Stefancic write,

---

1 Unless otherwise noted, all biblical texts are ESV.
2 Ibram X. Kendi, *Stamped from the Beginning: The Definitive History of Racist Ideas in America* (Bold Type Books, 2016), 1–2.

> Poverty ... has a black or brown face: black families command, on the average, about one-thirteenth of the assets of their white counterparts. They pay more for many products and services, including cars. People of color lead shorter lives, receive worse medical care, complete fewer years of school, and occupy more menial jobs than do whites.... Why all this is so and the relationship between racism and economic oppression—between race and class—are topics of great interest to critical race theory.[3]

Jemar Tisby asserts, "Racism today comes in the form of ... the ongoing and widening racial wealth gap."[4]

A common premise can be discerned from these statements: the idea that wealth and the good life go hand in hand, and the implication seems to be that some do not have wealth because of structural, societal injustice. On this point, Liz Mineo writes in the *Harvard Gazette*, "The wealth gap between Black and white Americans has been persistent and extreme. It represents, scholars say, the accumulated effects of four centuries of institutional and systemic racism and bears major responsibility for disparities in income, health, education, and opportunity that continue to this day."[5]

My goal in this presentation is to compare this premise (that wealth and the good life are necessarily connected) and its implication (that some do not have wealth because of structural injustice) to the teaching of Solomon in Ecclesiastes and Proverbs. This is an attempt to compare and contrast the worldviews of the Critical Race Theorists, on the one hand, and Solomon on the other. The majority of this paper will seek to exposit Solomon's worldview and how it impacts what he says about wealth. Whereas many advocates of social justice who speak to wealth in our culture seem

---

[3] Richard Delgado and Jean Stefancic, *Critical Race Theory: An Introduction*, 3rd ed. (New York University Press, 2017), 13.

[4] Jemar Tisby, *How to Fight Racism: Courageous Christianity and the Journey toward Racial Justice* (Zondervan, 2021), 31.

[5] Liz Mineo, "Racial Wealth Gap May Be a Key to Other Inequities," *Harvard Gazette* (blog), 3 June 2021, https://news.harvard.edu/gazette/story/2021/06/racial-wealth-gap-may-be-a-key-to-other-inequities/.

to suggest that racism accounts for why some have wealth and others do not, the perspective reflected in the two books of Solomon we will consider here is more nuanced and flexible on the questions of *the relative value* of wealth and *whether* it goes hand in hand with the good life.

I am working from evangelical assumptions about Proverbs and Ecclesiastes that, I think, largely nullify the purported difficulty of integrating the so-called Wisdom Literature with biblical theology. These evangelical assumptions include (but are not limited to) the following:

- that the attributions of most of the material in Proverbs to Solomon are true and that the reference to "the son of David, king in Jerusalem" who surpassed all before him in Ecclesiastes 1:1, 1:16, and 2:9 likewise point to Solomon;[6]
- that when Solomon speaks of his father teaching him in Proverbs 4:2–3, he refers to David obeying Deuteronomy 6 (esp. 6:4–7, along with 17:14–20);
- that as Solomon addresses his son throughout Proverbs he too seeks to obey Deuteronomy 6 and 17 in an effort to prepare the future king of Israel to do the same;
- that the idea that Solomon seeks to obey Deuteronomy 6 explains the heavy consonance between the teaching of Proverbs and Deuteronomy;
- that the idea that Solomon's teaching flows out of Deuteronomy

---

6 Contra R. N. Whybray, who writes, "It has long been recognized, however, that these attributions have no evidential value as far as *authorship* is concerned and do not necessarily indicate whose is the voice that speaks in these proverbs." R. N. Whybray, *Wealth and Poverty in the Book of Proverbs*, JSOTSupp 99 (JSOT, 1990), 46. It seems to me that the attributions to which Whybray alludes, at Prov 1:1; 10:1; and 25:1, carry significant evidential value regarding both authorship and the voice that speaks in the proverbs. The attributions are, after all, primary source material universally attested in all textual witnesses to the content of the book of Proverbs. On Solomon as author of both Proverbs and Ecclesiastes, see Duane A. Garrett, *Proverbs, Ecclesiastes, Song of Songs*, NAC 14 (Broadman and Holman, 1993), 52, 254–267. For Proverbs, see also Bruce K. Waltke, *The Book Of Proverbs: Chapters 1–15*, NICOT (Eerdmans, 2004), 31–37. For Ecclesiastes, see the case Fredericks makes in Daniel C. Fredericks and Daniel J. Estes, *Ecclesiastes and the Song of Songs*, ApOTC 16 (InterVarsity, 2010), 31–36.

indicates that he embraced the whole of the Torah and all other Scripture available to him;[7]
- and that this in turn requires us to read Proverbs and Ecclesiastes as reflections on and contributions to the covenantal and salvation historical worldview set forth in the Torah by Moses and built upon by the other biblical authors.[8]

What people say about wealth is a window into their worldview. According to Critical Race Theorists and Social Justice advocates, disparity in wealth results from the fact that "racism is ordinary, not aberrational ... the usual way society does business, the common, everyday experience of most people of color in this country."[9] It seems that according to this worldview, racism is the problem, and the wealth gap proves it.

In Solomon's scriptural worldview, by contrast, the problem is that man sinned against God, resulting in the Genesis 3:14–19 words of judgment. Because of sin, humanity has been forbidden access to the tree of life (Gen 3:22), expelled from Eden (3:23–24) to work the cursed land (3:17, 23), and all this under the sentence of death (2:17; 3:19). The resolution to this problem requires atonement being made for sin so that God can offer just forgiveness, and those who experience God's merciful salvation are reconciled to God. In the biblical worldview, life's highest good is not wealth but God's presence: "in your presence there is fullness of joy; at your right hand are pleasures forevermore" (Ps 16:11).

To be fair to the Critical Race Theorists, I would observe that they do not assert that their highest good is to possess wealth. But here I would critique their worldview against the standard of the Christian worldview. Whereas the Bible spells out the problem, its

---

[7] Scott Harris discusses Prov 1:8–19 and Gen 37, Prov 1:20–33 and Jer 7 and 20, and Prov 6:1–19 and the Joseph story. Scott L. Harris, *Proverbs 1–9: A Study of Inner-Biblical Interpretation*, SBLDS (Scholars Press, 1995).

[8] Whybray does not think that Solomon wrote Proverbs, nor does he interpret the book as teaching that flows out of the Torah of Moses, so it is not surprising that he thinks different statements made in the book reflect "different attitudes towards wealth and poverty" and "widely differing points of view." Whybray, *Wealth and Poverty in Proverbs*, 9–10.

[9] Delgado and Stefancic, *Critical Race Theory*, 8.

resolution, and what makes for a good life now and in the hereafter, Critical Race Theory does not spell out a way for people to experience forgiveness and reconciliation, nor does it articulate its vision for what constitutes the good life now and in the future. We are left to draw our own conclusions based on what its advocates say. Ibram X. Kendi asserts, "The only remedy to racist discrimination is antiracist discrimination. The only remedy to past discrimination is present discrimination. The only remedy to present discrimination is future discrimination."[10] It appears that what is desired is power—power to discriminate, power to amass wealth, power to punish past wrongs. I submit that in Proverbs and Ecclesiastes Solomon shows us a more excellent way.

The wisdom that Solomon teaches stands most in contrast with the Critical Race Theory (CRT) worldview on the question of ultimate ends: everything Solomon says indicates that for him knowing God and enjoying him forever is the chief end of life, and this shows up in the way God is a non-factor for those who operate according to CRT.

The Covenant and Salvation History

In the tradition Solomon was taught, which he also propagated, a tradition stemming from the Torah of Moses, *the* blessing of the covenant is life with God. Yahweh promises in Leviticus 26:11-13 that he will walk among his people as he walked in the garden, that he will dwell with them, that they will be his people and he will be their God. Because of who he is, the life-giving creator, fulness of life is found in his presence. If he is present with his people, life and blessing will abound for them because that's what happens where he is. Thus the blessings of the covenant in Leviticus 26: the land will have rain in season and be abundantly fruitful, almost like the garden of Eden before sin (Lev 26:3-5). The protection of his presence will also keep his people, the seed of the woman, from the enmity directed against them by their enemies, the seed

---

10 Ibram X. Kendi, "Book Extract: Ibram X. Kendi Defines What It Means to Be an Antiracist," Penguin Books, 9 June 2020, https://www.penguin.co.uk/articles/2020/june/ibram-x-kendi-definition-of-antiracist.html.

of the serpent, as well as from harmful beasts (26:6–8). In addition to the promises that pertain to land and blessing, God promises to make his people fruitful and multiply them (26:9), giving them offspring, or seed. The blessings of the covenant, then, promise realization of God's promises to Abraham (Gen 12:1–3). The best part, of course, is that God promises himself to his people, his own presence (Lev 26:11–13).

Adam and Eve sinned and were driven from God's presence. When God declares that Israel is his son (Exod 4:22–23), he asserts that the nation is a new Adam. Having liberated his new-Adam son from slavery in Egypt, he brings Israel to the land of promise, a new Eden where they are to enjoy God's presence in accordance with the terms of God's covenant. Israel's master story, the story that begins in the Torah of Moses, feeds into a distinctive worldview that cannot be simply equated with the alternative worldviews held by those who worshiped other gods and interpreted life according to other master narratives.[11]

Israel's master story traces a line of descent from Adam and Eve, to whom the conquering seed of the woman was promised in Genesis 3:15, through the genealogies to Noah (Gen 5), to Abraham (Gen 11), to David, and the covenant Yahweh makes with David in 2 Samuel 7 indicates that the blessing of Abraham will be realized through the future king from David's line. Solomon, the first king from David's line, reigns as a new-Adam, representative Israelite, exercising dominion, teaching wisdom, a type of the one to come.[12] It is in this covenantal and salvation historical setting that the books of Proverbs and Ecclesiastes must be interpreted.

From what Solomon says in Proverbs and Ecclesiastes, I would

---

11 Because he fails to understand this point about the distinctive covenantal and salvation historical worldview of the biblical authors, including Solomon, Whybray writes, "The speakers [in Proverbs] share the view common to their ancient Near Eastern civilizations that wealth is, generally speaking, a blessing—though some qualify this assessment in various ways." Whybray, *Wealth and Poverty in Proverbs*, 113. On the contrary, only Israel was in covenant with Yahweh, and Yahweh only promised the blessings of the covenant to Israel. We must understand that the blessing of wealth in Proverbs is a particularly *covenantal* blessing.

12 See further James M. Hamilton, *Typology—Understanding the Bible's Promise-Shaped Patterns: How Old Testament Expectations Are Fulfilled in Christ* (Zondervan, 2022).

propose that we can see his statements in their wider context by articulating the question he seems to be answering in each respective book.

In Proverbs, it is as though Solomon is answering the question: how does one enter the garden of Eden to enjoy the presence of God?

In Ecclesiastes, it is as though Solomon answers the question: since all die, what is good for man to do?[13]

Proverbs: Wisdom to Enter Eden

If life's *summum bonum* is the presence of God, then measuring quality of life by economic standing would seem to imply that God sells time in his presence to the highest bidder. But if cash will not purchase a place in God's presence, we need some other index by which to assess quality of life. Solomon teaches his son that far more valuable than the possession of currency is the experience of knowing God and experiencing God's blessing, so he urges his son to get wisdom, the wisdom that knows to seek God.

Approaching the material from this covenantal and salvation historical perspective, informed by the teaching of Torah and the identity of the author, knowing his responsibilities to teach Torah to his son, who will one day be king, we can understand why Solomon would set out to write a book "to give prudence to the simple, knowledge and discretion to the youth" (Prov 1:4). Young simpletons—and sometimes older people with no lack of shrewdness—are tempted to think that money is the key to life's pleasures. Get the key; unlock the pleasures.

Solomon makes a deeply personal appeal to the strongest of relational and affectional bonds when he pleads with his son to hear his father's instruction and forsake not his mother's *Torah* (Prov 1:8), promising adornment characterized by God's own gracious character (חֵן, 1:9). As his father David taught, so Solomon urges against "the counsel of the wicked" (Ps 1:3) as he seeks to

---

[13] The center of Solomon's theology is the glory of God in salvation through judgment. See the discussion in James M. Hamilton Jr., *God's Glory in Salvation through Judgment: A Biblical Theology* (Crossway, 2010), 290–301, 313–320.

deconstruct the allurement of sinners by showing the outcome of their attempt to make breaking the commandments (not to murder and not to steal) attractive (Prov 1:10–19). David taught that "the way of the wicked will perish" (Ps 1:6), and Solomon likewise asserts that loss of life awaits those who seek life by gaining treasure through murder and theft (Prov 1:18–19).

Wisdom in Proverbs is not merely an impersonal force that punishes the wicked and rewards the righteous. No, wisdom begins with the recognition that God himself personally polices the commandments he gave about how his created order is to be stewarded. And this is not some abstract deity but Yahweh, covenant God of Israel. Thus, "The fear of Yahweh is the beginning of knowledge" (Prov 1:7), and those who refuse the call of personified wisdom have "hated knowledge" and not chosen "the fear of Yahweh" (1:29).

What Solomon wants most for his son is for him to have such an experience of God that he will know God and that his confidence in God's holy character and faithful commitment to upholding his own word will make the prospect of transgression terrifying because of the certain judgment that will ensue. Accordingly, Solomon urges his son to receive his words, treasure his commandments, make his ear attentive to wisdom, incline his heart to understanding, call out for insight, raise his voice for understanding, and seek this understanding like silver, searching for it as for hidden treasure (Prov 2:1–4)—because this understanding, *not money*, is the key that unlocks the door to the good life—"then you will understand the fear of Yahweh and find the knowledge of God" (2:5).

Solomon's teaching in Proverbs assumes earlier Scripture. His statements depend upon shared knowledge between himself and his audience. He does not spell things out, as I am doing here, because he does not think he needs to make the connections overt. He knows the context in which his son, and the other members of his audience, operate.

Thus Solomon does not feel a need to remind his audience that God promised land, seed, and blessing to Abraham (Gen 12:1–3), and that the Ten Commandments exposit the character of Yahweh as he proclaimed himself to Moses in Exodus 34:6–7, with the rest of the Torah's stipulations being understood as expositions of the umbrella statement of those Ten Words.

Solomon does not need to restate all this in the same way that when Joe Buck goes to the microphone for a World Series broadcast, he doesn't proceed to explain baseball as though his audience is watching their first game. Joe Buck assumes that his audience understands how the game works. Solomon does the same.

Land was promised to Abraham, however, and in the same way Adam was exiled from Eden, the curses of the covenant God made with Israel through Moses warn of exile from the land of promise. As Solomon urges his son—not literally but metaphorically—to stay on the straight and narrow path that leads to life that he might re-enter Eden (cf. Prov 2:20), he explains, "For the upright will inhabit the land, and those with integrity will remain in it, but the wicked will be cut off from the land, and the treacherous will be rooted out of it" (2:21–22). When Solomon promises that wisdom will be "a tree of life to those who lay hold of her" (3:18), it is almost as though wisdom takes people into the garden of Eden. Along these lines, the teaching of the righteous, the fear of Yahweh, and good sense are all said to be a fountain of life (10:11; 13:14; 14:27; 16:22; cf. Ps 36:9).

Before we consider the way Solomon presents the teaching of Torah as the expression of God's character and the path to experiencing the good life by enjoying God's presence and blessing in Proverbs 3, allow me to give examples of statements that articulate the two other aspects of the blessing of Abraham: seed and blessing. We see the concern for seed in statements such as Proverbs 13:22: "A good man leaves an inheritance to his children's children, but the sinner's wealth is laid up for the righteous." And the promise of blessing stands crisply in 10:22: "The blessing of the LORD makes rich, and he adds no sorrow with it."

Some relevant aspects of the Torah, such as the blessing of Abraham (Gen 12:1–3) and Yahweh's declaration of his own name and character (Exod 34:6–7), have been briefly referenced above. To appreciate what Solomon says in Proverbs 3, we should also note the way that in the Torah Moses gives certain pieces of financial instruction that are, to put it mildly, counterintuitive. Parade examples of what I have in mind relate to the sabbatical year, which required that every seventh year Israel give the land a Sabbath (Lev 25:1–7), neither sowing the field or pruning the vineyard (25:4). Though potential objections about how the people will be provided for are addressed (25:20–22), Yahweh seems to know that the people will not let the land lie fallow, promising that the land will have the sabbaths the people refused to give it once they have definitively broken the covenant and been driven into exile (26:34–35).

Not only were the people instructed not to work on the seventh year, they were instructed to release the debts of their fellow Israelites in the seventh year (Deut 15:1–6), and they were specifically told not to refuse to lend money because the seventh year was near (15:7–11). I submit that these two regulations, the sabbatical year and the release of debts to Israelites in the same, would have to be obeyed by faith. That is, as both Leviticus 25 and Deuteronomy 15 promise, the people would have to trust the Lord to provide and bless in spite of the fact that, considered by worldly standards, it would make no financial sense to follow these instructions.

Enter Solomon to teach his son in Proverbs 3:1–12. This unit of Proverbs 3 has a chiastic structure that can be depicted as follows:[14]

    3:1–2: My son, keep Torah for long life
        3:3–4: Yahweh's character results in favor and success
            3:5–6: Trust and know Yahweh
            3:7–8: Fear Yahweh for healing refreshment
        3:9–10: Honoring Yahweh with wealth produces abundance
    3:11–12: My son, the Lord disciplines those he loves

In this chiastic structure, the fatherly instruction in Torah that leads to long life in Proverbs 3:1–2 stands across from the 3:11–12 fatherly discipline by Yahweh of those he loves—in terms reminiscent of the discipline of the Davidic king from 2 Samuel 7:14. And

---

14 See also the chiastic structure for the whole of Proverbs 3 proposed in James M. Hamilton Jr., "That the Coming Generation Might Praise the Lord," *Journal of Family Ministry* 1, no. 1 (2010): 17.

for the purposes of this study, we note that the call to live out God's own character of "steadfast love and faithfulness" (חֶסֶד וֶאֱמֶת) in Proverbs 3:3–4 stands across from the faith-based honoring of God with wealth in 3:9–10. Godliness results in a God-honoring use of wealth. At the center of this chiastic structure stands the two-sided coin of trusting and knowing Yahweh on the one hand and fearing him and not being wise in one's own eyes on the other.

In this passage, Solomon teaches his son that obeying Torah leads to life and *shalom* (Prov 3:1–2). In Deuteronomy 6:6 Moses tells Israel that his words are to be on their hearts, in 6:7 he tells them to teach his words to their sons, and then in 6:8 he tells them—metaphorically—to bind (קָשַׁר) the words as a sign on their hand. Similarly, in Proverbs 3:1 Solomon instructs *his son* to keep his words *in his heart*, promising the same thing Moses promised to those who obey: long life (Deut 6:2; Prov 3:2).[15] Solomon then metaphorically tells his son to do the same thing with God's "steadfast love and faithfulness" (חֶסֶד וֶאֱמֶת) that Moses said to do with the word: bind it, but here not on the hand but around the neck. And in anticipation of Jeremiah 31:33, Solomon instructs his son to *write on the tablet of his heart* what he is teaching him: *Torah*, commandments, steadfast love and faithfulness. In my view, Solomon in Proverbs repackages the teaching of Torah in memorable ways for the instruction of his son, and by extension for all those under his fatherly kingship (all the people of God). I would note as well, though, that for Solomon to tell his son to do the same thing with his teaching that Moses told his audience to do with the Torah seems tantamount to Solomon indicating that his teaching carries the same level of authority as that of Moses. In other words, Solomon seems to think that he is writing instruction that comes from God and is to be regarded as Scripture.

As we have seen, some of the financial instructions in the Torah will seem counterintuitive, and other aspects certainly go against sinful inclinations humans have—greedy impulses that result in exploitative financial practices,[16] whether those relate to acquisition

---

15 See the table depicting lexical points of contact between Deuteronomy 6 and 17 and Proverbs 3 in Hamilton, "Coming Generation," 17–18.

16 Cf. Prov 28:25: "A greedy man stirs up strife, but the one who trusts in the

of land, the charging of interest, or other matters Moses addresses in the Torah.[17] Anticipating the all too human impulse to acquire excessive silver and gold, which the king was expressly forbidden from doing in Deuteronomy 17:17, Solomon urges his son to trust Yahweh with his whole heart and not to lean on his own understanding (Prov 3:5), to know Yahweh in all his ways and be directed by him in all his paths (3:6).

Solomon knows exactly what his son needs if he is to obey this instruction: he needs to be not wise in his own eyes, to fear Yahweh and turn from evil (3:7), and Solomon makes promises reminiscent of things his father David said in Psalm 19:7 ("reviving the soul") and Psalm 32 (relief from bones wasting away), saying that fearing Yahweh will be healing to flesh and refreshment to bones (Prov 3:8).

In this context, having urged his son to trust, know, and fear Yahweh, centering that instruction in the chiastic structure of Proverbs 3:1–12, having taught that the Torah leads to life and *shalom* (3:1–2), that living out the Torah by enacting God's character (3:3) leads to favor and success in the sight of God and man (3:4; cf. Luke 2:52), Solomon teaches his son to honor Yahweh with his wealth, promising that doing so will lead to God's covenant blessings on field and vineyard (Prov 3:9–10).

More could undoubtedly be said, but I contend that in Proverbs Solomon teaches his son how to pursue the good life, and that good life consists of trusting, knowing, and fearing Yahweh, living in accordance with his character as revealed in the commands and prohibitions, instructions, and regulations given in the Torah of Moses. Living this way will not *literally* take one back into the garden of Eden, but the best thing about the garden was the presence of God. In the tabernacle and temple Yahweh gave to Israel a Leviticult that would enable them to experience his presence and not be struck dead by his holiness. Solomon urges his son to embrace the wisdom of living in accordance with Torah, in the fear of Yahweh, to know him and enjoy his presence.

Lord will be enriched."

17 Consider, for instance, Prov 28:8: "Whoever multiplies his wealth by interest and profit gathers it for him who is generous to the poor."

What Solomon says reflects no divide between Torah and wisdom.[18] Rather, the same thing David said about the man who delights in Torah in Psalm 1:1, 3—that he would be blessed (אַשְׁרֵי־הָאִישׁ; "blessed is the man")—Solomon says of the one who finds wisdom in Proverbs 3:13 (אַשְׁרֵי אָדָם; "blessed is the man"). He goes on to explain that the one who finds wisdom and gets understanding (Prov 3:13) has acquired something that will produce better yield than the profits of silver and gold (3:14) because wisdom is "more precious than jewels, and nothing you desire can compare with her" (3:15). She has long life in her right hand, riches and honor in her left (3:16), and her ways are pleasant, her paths *shalom* (3:17). Those who have wisdom are called "blessed" (מְאֻשָּׁר).

We turn our attention to Ecclesiastes, the "words of delight" and "words of truth" (Eccl 12:10) that Solomon gave "like goads," "like nails firmly fixed" from the "one Shepherd" (12:11). This "one Shepherd" by whom "the words of the wise" and "the collected sayings" are given seems to be God,[19] so here again it seems that Solomon claims that what he has written in Ecclesiastes is the word of God.

Ecclesiastes: Doing Good in the Face of Death

In the book of Ecclesiastes Solomon provides mankind with our deepest exploration of what death means for human life. Death, the consequence warned of in Genesis 2:17, then visited on humanity after sin (Gen 3:19; Rom 5:12), is arguably the driving reality behind the assessment that brackets Solomon's meditation: "Vanity of vanities, says the Preacher, vanity of vanities! All is vanity (Eccl 1:2; 12:8).

The fact that death awaits us all gives urgency to the question Solomon raises in Ecclesiastes 1:3, a question that immediately puts the social-justice-premise to the test: "What does a man

---

18 Contra Duane A. Garrett, *The Problem of the Old Testament: Hermeneutical, Schematic, and Theological Approaches* (InterVarsity, 2020), 165–170.

19 James Bollhagen, *Ecclesiastes*, ConcC (Saint Louis: Concordia, 2011), 432; Garrett, *Proverbs, Ecclesiastes, Song of Songs*, 344.

gain by all the toil at which he toils under the sun?"[20] The end that looms over all puts Solomon on the quest to seek "what was good for the children of man to do under heaven during the few days of their life" (Eccl 2:3).[21] Death means that pleasure (2:1–11) and wisdom (2:12–17) are but "vanity and a striving after wind" (2:11, 17; see esp. 2:14–16). Death results in the frustrations of having to leave the results of wisdom and skill to one who might be a fool (2:18–26). There is a time for everything (3:1–8), and the question of what is to be gained by toil remains (3:9). God has made everything beautiful in its time and put eternity in man's heart (3:11), and Solomon looks God's justice (3:17) full in the face: as man was made from dust in Genesis 2:7 and sentenced to return to it in 3:19, the vanity of Ecclesiastes 3:19 arises from the fact that, as stated in 3:20, "All go to one place. All are from the dust, and to dust all return" (cf. 12:7). Solomon wrestles with the problem of solitude (4:7–16), and his ruminations on having and enjoying in chapters 5 and 6 are particularly relevant for the topic of this paper.

As he continues to pursue the question of what is good for man to do (Eccl 6:12), he turns to consider the way that man is unable to fully understand God's work (6:10–11:6, see esp. 8:17; 11:5–6; cf. 3:11). We do not always know what is best to do, and we do not know what will come after (6:12). Decline and death, however, should be considered that the living might gain wisdom (11:7–12:8).

How does Solomon in his wisdom recommend that people respond to the fact that death makes everything vanity and a striving after wind? To answer this question, the whole book must be taken together, and no *sachkritik* should be used to excise portions of the book, nor should we attribute the epilogue to some other author. In his conclusion Solomon affirms key ideas that he has peppered throughout his discourse: "The end of the matter; all has been heard. Fear God and keep his commandments, for this is the

---

20 A slightly altered form of the question recurs in Eccl 3:9.
21 Though I do not directly cite him here, my thinking on Ecclesiastes has been shaped by Addison G. Wright, "The Riddle of the Sphinx: The Structure of the Book of Qoheleth," *CBQ* 30 (1968): 313–334; idem, "The Riddle of the Sphinx Revisited: Numerical Patterns in the Book of Qoheleth," *CBQ* 42 (1980): 38–51; idem, "Additional Numerical Patterns in Qoheleth," *CBQ* 45 (1983): 32–43.

whole duty of man. For God will bring every deed into judgment, with every secret thing, whether good or evil" (Eccl 12:13–14).

Note that Solomon has just warned young men that as they enjoy their youthful vigor they should remember that God will bring them into judgment for all these things (Eccl 11:9). Though he does not say the words "fear Yahweh," surely the call to remember that God will judge is meant to stimulate appropriate caution, reverence, circumspection, and to put it positively, a commitment to walk in the safe space of obedience because of the fear of judgment.

Solomon likewise asserted in Ecclesiastes 8:12–13, "Though a sinner does evil a hundred times and prolongs his life, yet I know that it will be well with those who fear God, because they fear before him. But it will not be well with the wicked, neither will he prolong his days like a shadow, because he does not fear before God."

He also urges the fear of God in Ecclesiastes 3:14 and 5:7, warning of judgment in 3:17 and, implicitly, in all the references to death and the consequences of not pleasing God. The application of these ideas to how to approach the good life can be seen in the repeated encouragement to enjoy what God gives in the form of food, drink, labor, and family life (Eccl 2:24–25; 3:12–13, 22; 5:18; 8:13; 9:7–10; 11:8–10; cf. Ps 128). One way that Solomon aids his audience in getting to a mindset that enables them to live out his teaching can be seen in his emphasis on the fact that the ability to enjoy is a gift of God not given to all.

The futility of wealth can be particularly felt as Solomon writes in Ecclesiastes 6:1–2, "There is an evil that I have seen under the sun, and it lies heavy on mankind: a man to whom God gives wealth, possessions, and honor, so that he lacks nothing of all that he desires, yet God does not give him power to enjoy them, but a stranger enjoys them. This is vanity; it is a grievous evil."

One aspect of the gift of the power to enjoy wealth surely involves contentment, which overcomes the insatiability Solomon describes as afflicting mankind: Ecclesiastes 1:8b, "the eye is not satisfied with seeing, nor the ear filled with hearing;" 3:11, "he has put eternity into man's heart;" 4:8, "his eyes are never satisfied with riches;" 5:10, "he who loves money will not be satisfied with money, nor he who loves wealth with his income."

Solomon knows there is injustice in the world (3:16; 4:1; 5:8; 7:7), and he knows that in worldly terms "money answers everything" (10:19). And still his positive message is that God's gift is to enjoy one's work and the blessings of the covenant, and as in Proverbs, he commends diligence: "But this is gain for a land in every way: a king committed to cultivated fields" (5:9).

Conclusion

What Solomon teaches about wealth and poverty in Proverbs and Ecclesiastes is fruit that grows on a tree planted by the Torah stream, in the sunshine of the teaching of David, informed by the other prophets who had been active to that point. Consider, for instance, how what Solomon says resonates both with what Moses said in Deuteronomy 8:17–18 and Hannah's prayer in 1 Samuel 2:7:

> Beware lest you say in your heart, "My power and the might of my hand have gotten me this wealth." You shall remember the LORD your God, for it is he who gives you power to get wealth, that he may confirm his covenant that he swore to your fathers, as it is this day. (Deut 8:17–18)

> The LORD makes poor and makes rich; he brings low and exalts. (1 Sam 2:7)

This perspective can also be seen to inform the Lord Jesus in his disregard for earthly wealth and happy embrace of economic poverty. As Paul puts it in 2 Corinthians 8:9, "For you know the grace of our Lord Jesus Christ, that though he was rich, yet for your sake he became poor, so that you by his poverty might become rich." Paul likewise knew a joy in God that did not arise from money: "I know how to be brought low, and I know how to abound. In any and every circumstance, I have learned the secret of facing plenty and hunger, abundance and need" (Phil 4:12).

We have good news both for those who have embraced Critical Race Theory and for those who in their desire for social justice demand equal outcomes for all: there is a good and wise God who can be trusted to administrate all economic outcomes according to his good pleasure. It has not been given to us to control those outcomes, for the secret things belong to him (Deut 29:29). What has been given to us is a revealed call to learn wisdom, to see the futility of living to amass wealth, experience earthly pleasure, or gain power—nor does Solomon commend all-consuming advocacy of justice in the here and now as the path to the good life (cf. Eccl 3:16–17). The wisdom that Solomon teaches urges us to know God, to trust him, to fear him, and to enjoy his goodness to us. That is his gift to us.

3

"Provided We Suffer with Him": A Pauline Theology of Suffering and the Prosperity Gospel

Michael E. Pohlman

On July 18, 2021, prosperity preacher Casey Treat delivered a sermon to his Seattle megachurch (founded 1980) titled "Force of Faith." He began by informing his audience of "two things that changed everything in my life" at the age of nineteen when he experienced a conversion to Christianity in a drug rehabilitation center. The two things were needed to renew his mind according to Scripture and to use his faith so that he would "not be limited by this world." Treat explained, "That's how [my wife] Wendy and I are celebrating our forty years of marriage, healthy and strong and whole. Yesterday we were out on our bicycles, rode for twenty-five miles and we said, 'It's still working! It's still working!'" Treat went on to credit prosperity pastors Julius Young and Frederick Price, his two "spiritual fathers in the faith," with teaching him these spiritual techniques to "leave my depressions, fears, anxieties, addictions, poverty—all of that, behind."[1]

The Prosperity Gospel

Not only is the prosperity gospel "still working" for Casey and Wendy Treat, but based on the proliferation of it not only in America but around the world, it's still working for millions of other people as well. Consider the American context alone. According to Kate Bowler in *Blessed: A History of the American Prosperity Gospel*, in 2011 one million people were attending American prosperity

---

[1] Casey Treat, "Force of Faith," Christian Faith, 18 July 2021, video, 40:32, https://christianfaith.us/archive/force-of-faith-casey-treat.

megachurches with the largest of these churches, Joel Osteen's Lakewood Church in Houston, boasting 38,000 members.[2] Some of the most recognized names in American Christianity over the last one hundred years are associated in one form or another with the prosperity gospel. Names like Oral Roberts, Kenneth Hagen, Kenneth Copeland, Frederick Price, John Hagee, Joyce Meyer, T. D. Jakes, Joel Osteen, and Creflo Dollar to name several. Institutions such as Oral Roberts University and Rhema Bible Training Center (part of Kenneth Hagen's ministry empire) have given the movement national recognition and served as somewhat of a unifying force among the many disparate prosperity gospel churches spread throughout America. Not only are prosperity churches and ministries not geographically limited but also prosperity preaching translates well into all the major media whether print, radio, television, or internet. Indeed, as Casey Treat declared, the prosperity gospel is "still working."

It's one thing to describe the ubiquity of the prosperity gospel but quite another to explain it. What exactly is the prosperity gospel? "Though it is hard to describe," observes Bowler, "it is easy to find. The prosperity gospel is a wildly popular Christian message of spiritual, physical, and financial mastery that dominates not only much of the American religious scene but some of the largest churches around the globe."[3] While the prosperity gospel has spread throughout the world, it has its roots in American soil. Indeed, it is in many ways the Americanization of Christianity. Bowler explains how the prosperity gospel is a particular "American blessing": "But rather than sacralizing the founding of the United States or visions of manifest destiny, the prosperity gospel was constituted by the deification and ritualization of the American Dream: upward mobility, accumulation, hard work, and moral fiber."[4] Its global persistence, however, is due to more than the appeal of the American Dream. After all, the American Dream doesn't explain the prosperity gospel's proliferation in a

---

2 Kate Bowler, *Blessed: A History of the American Prosperity Gospel* (Oxford University Press, 2013), 181.
3 Bowler, *Blessed*, 3.
4 Bowler, *Blessed*, 226.

place like Ethiopia where it's every bit as popular as it is in America. It has to do with its "comprehensive approach to the human condition":

> Why has it become so successful in so many places? We must not think that it is simply the lure of financial success. The prosperity movement offers a comprehensive approach to the human condition. It sees men and women as creatures fallen, but not broken, and it shares with them a "gospel," good news that will set them free from a multitude of oppressions .... The prosperity gospel's chief allure is simply optimism.[5]

What began as a baptized American Dream became the comprehensive answer to the human condition since the fall. A movement hatched inside Pentecostalism in the early twentieth century "soon found that its universal reassurances could carry it far beyond any denominational or sectarian home."[6] A global movement was born.

Surprisingly, given its dominance within American religion and global Christianity, the prosperity gospel has received scant scholarly attention.[7] It has become clear that the prosperity gospel is here to stay. Therefore, further study of the prosperity gospel is needed in the light of Scripture. In this chapter, I argue that the prosperity gospel is inconsistent with a Pauline theology of suffering. More specifically, when a Pauline theology of suffering is seen in its connection to glory, the prosperity gospel is seen for what it truly is, namely, a different gospel, which is really no gospel at all (see Gal 1:6–9).

---

5 Bowler, *Blessed*, 232.

6 Bowler, *Blessed*, 42.

7 While much scholarly attention in the twenty-first century has been given to relatively small religious movements in America like Christian Nationalism, Kate Bowler (*Blessed*) seems to be alone in her scholarly work on the prosperity gospel. The reasons for this may have to do with the lack of transparency the various prosperity ministries practice making it difficult for outsiders to research particular churches or ministers. Or, perhaps, prosperity gospel preachers are not deemed serious objects of study given their charlatan persona and thereby underestimating their influence.

A Pauline Theology of Suffering

In John Bunyan's classic allegory of the Christian life *The Pilgrim's Progress* the main character, Christian, soon after coming to the cross and having his burden removed, finds himself at the foot of Difficulty Hill. Joining him are two fellow travelers, Formalist and Hypocrisy. As the three gaze upon the Hill with its steep, treacherous terrain, both Formalist and Hypocrisy think better of going straight up its face opting to take two easier paths around the base of the Hill. Formalist chooses the path to the left called Danger while Hypocrisy chooses the path to the right called Destruction. Both paths live up to their name as Formalist perishes in a dark wood, and Hypocrisy falls to his death over a steep cliff. Christian, meanwhile, proceeds up the face of Difficulty Hill at first running along rather effortlessly. But this would soon change as Christian's running slows to a crawl on his hands and knees as he, with great difficulty, finally makes it to a pleasant arbor, a place of refreshment provided by the King for weary travelers.

It is significant that Bunyan introduces Christian to the Hill of Difficulty shortly after having his burden removed at the cross. For Bunyan knows that this is the way to the Celestial City, and Christian would need to learn this sooner rather than later. Indeed, not only did his journey not become *easier* after having his burden removed, it actually become *harder*. And this is where the prosperity gospel goes so tragically amiss by depicting Christianity as a faith without Difficulty Hill.

One of the clearest biblical texts that undermines the prosperity gospel is Romans 8:12–17. For in this passage, we see the apostle Paul's teaching about the necessity of suffering in the Christian life. It reads,

> So then, brothers, we are debtors, not to the flesh, to live according to the flesh. For if you live according to the flesh you will die, but if by the Spirit you put to death the deeds of the body, you will live. For all who are led by the Spirit of God are sons of God. For you did not receive the spirit of slavery to fall back into fear, but you have received the Spirit of adoption as

sons, by whom we cry, "Abba! Father!" The Spirit himself bears witness with our spirit that we are children of God, and if children, then heirs—heirs of God and fellow heirs with Christ, provided we suffer with him in order that we may also be glorified with him.[8]

Paul begins this pericope by demonstrating that a Christian does not live "according to the flesh" (v. 12). That is, Christians do not live under the tyranny or mastery or dominion of sin. As he explained earlier in chapter 8, "There is therefore now no condemnation for those who are in Christ Jesus. For the law of the Spirit of life has set you free in Christ Jesus from the law of sin and death" (vv. 1–2). The Christian's freedom in Christ makes living according to the flesh impossible. This is a theme the apostle took up in chapter six when he asked, "What shall we say then? Are we to continue in sin that grace may abound? By no means! How can we who died to sin still live in it?... We know that our old self was crucified with him in order that the body of sin might be brought to nothing, so that we would no longer be enslaved to sin. For one who has died to sin has been set free from sin" (6:1–2, 6–7). The Christian is a debtor not to the flesh but to the Spirit. Knowing this is of utmost importance given that eternity is at stake: "For if you live according to the flesh you will die, but if by the Spirit you put to death the deeds of the body, you will live" (8:13).

Children of God

Having established that Christians are Spirit-led people, the apostle proceeds to outline what is the true identity of a Christian, namely, a child of God: "For all who are led by the Spirit of God are sons of God. For you did not receive the spirit of slavery to fall back into fear, but you have received the Spirit of adoption as sons, by whom we cry, 'Abba! Father!'" (vv. 14–15). If you are led by the Spirit of God—that is, if you're a Christian—then you are a child of God. No slavery to sin with corresponding fear of judgment as we saw earlier in Romans 8:1. We now "put to death the deeds

---

8 Unless otherwise noted, all scripture quotations come from the ESV.

of the body" by relating to God as our benevolent Father. In the battle against sin, we cry out to God in the most personal of ways, "Abba! Father!" Just how personal is this address? Consider that it is the same address Jesus used in Gethsemane on the eve of his crucifixion as he prayed, "Abba, Father, all things are possible for you. Remove this cup from me. Yet not what I will, but what you will" (Mark 14:36). As a child of God, the Christian has the privilege of approaching the Father in the same intimate way as the Son of God.

How does the Christian come to declare this? Paul explains something of the mystery of the inward testimony of the Holy Spirit in the believer: "The Spirit himself bears witness with our spirit that we are children of God" (Rom 8:16). In verse 15 we're told that by the Spirit *we* cry "Abba! Father!" We cry out *as the Spirit bears witness to us* of our true identity as children of God. The Spirit testifies to us that we can approach God knowing that when we do, we will find not a wrathful judge but a gracious Father.

Fellow Heirs with Christ

To deepen our assurance, Paul draws out a profound implication of being children of God: "and if children, then heirs—heirs of God and fellow heirs with Christ" (v. 17). What does it mean to be a "fellow heir" with Christ? Or, to ask it differently, what is Christ's inheritance? In a word, everything. We see this clearly in the opening verses of the book of Hebrews: "Long ago, at many times and in many ways, God spoke to our fathers by the prophets, but in these last days he has spoken to us by his Son, whom he appointed the heir of all things, through whom also he created the world" (Heb 1:1–2; cf. Matt 28:18; Phil 2:9). In fulfillment of Psalm 2, the nations are his heritage, the ends of the earth his possession. Indeed, every beast of the forest is his, the cattle on a thousand hills (Ps 50:10).

As a fellow heir with Christ, everything that is Christ's is the Christian's. This is the argument Paul uses in 1 Corinthians 3 when he's chastising the church for the evident "jealously and strife" among them as they were lining up behind their favorite leader. Divisions were developing as "one says, 'I follow Paul,' and another, 'I follow Apollos'" (vv. 3–4). To this Paul reasons, "So let no one boast in men. For all things are yours, whether Paul or Apollos or Cephas or the world or life or death or the present or the future—all are yours, and you are Christ's, and Christ is God's" (vv. 21–23). Why, in other words, would you boast in men when everything that is Christ's is yours? Of course, this inheritance is of infinite worth because at its heart is God—it will be the glorious fulfillment of the new covenant promise: "you shall be my people and I will be your God" (Ezek 36:28; cf. Luke 12:32).

A Necessary Condition

Having explained the Christian's identity as a child of God and co-heir with Christ, the apostle adds a necessary condition: "and if children, then heirs—heirs of God and fellow heirs with Christ, *provided* we suffer with him in order that we may also be glorified with him" (Rom 8:17; italics added). The Greek word translated "provided" ("if indeed" in the NIV/NASB) is the conditional particle εἴπερ (*eiper*), indicating a real condition that must be fulfilled by anyone who would be an heir.[9] And the condition that must be fulfilled is suffering.

The Greek word used in Romans 8:17 translated "we suffer with" is συμπάσχομεν (*sympaschomen*), meaning "to share in suffering." Moisés Silva glosses it "to suffer the same as, suffer with."[10] William Mounce similarly glosses it "to suffer as another," "endure corresponding sufferings."[11] This suffering is "to feel or endure distress."[12] And we do this in solidarity with Christ and his sufferings. It is, as Paul says in Philippians 3:10, a "fellowship in his sufferings." And it is important to note that the word is a *present active indicative* meaning that this suffering is not a one-time event but an ongoing *condition* for the Christian this side of heaven.

The experience of suffering here is similar to the idea Paul

---

9 For other uses of the conditional participle εἴπερ, see Rom 3:30; 8:9; 1 Cor 8:5; 15:15; 2 Thess 1:6.

10 *NIDNTTE*, 3:666.

11 William D. Mounce, *The Analytical Lexicon of the Greek New Testament* (Zondervan, 1993), 430.

12 *NIDNTTE*, 3:666.

develops later in Romans 8 when he speaks of our "groaning." After noting that "the whole creation has been groaning together in the pains of childbirth until now" (v. 22), the apostle explains that God's people are likewise "groaning" under the curse of sin: "And not only the creation, but we ourselves, who have the firstfruits of the Spirit, groan inwardly as we wait eagerly for adoption as sons, the redemption of our bodies" (v. 23).[13] Mounce glosses "groan" (στενάζομεν) as "to groan, sigh."[14] Paul takes up this idea of groaning in 2 Corinthians 5:2–4 where he considers the ongoing burden of waiting for our final salvation:

> For in this tent we groan [στενάζομεν], longing to put on our heavenly dwelling, if indeed by putting it on we may not be found naked. For while we are still in this tent, we groan [στενάζομεν], being burdened—not that we would be unclothed, but that we would be further clothed, so that what is mortal may be swallowed up by life.

This groaning, this suffering, is the *normal, perpetual* condition of the Christian as we live this pilgrim life on our way to the Celestial City. After all, Paul says, "while we are still in this tent," that is, while we live in this body, "we groan, being burdened" (2 Cor 5:4).[15]

The Design of God

What the prosperity preachers fail to see (or willfully neglect) is the design of God in the Christian's suffering. They do not sufficiently appreciate the all-important conjunction ἵνα (*hina*) in Romans 8:17: "*in order that* we may also be glorified with him" (italics added). The purpose or design behind our suffering is glory (a

---

13 N.B. the *already* and *not yet* of Paul's theology: we have *already* the "fristfruits of the Spirit" even as we "groan inwardly as we wait" for the *not yet* of our final salvation, the "redemption of our bodies."

14 Mounce, *Analytical Lexicon*, 422.

15 Cf. 1 Pet 4:12–13: "Beloved, do not be surprised at the fiery trial when it comes upon you to test you, as though something strange were happening to you. But rejoice insofar as you share Christ's sufferings, that you may also rejoice and be glad when his glory is revealed."

restatement of "inheritance"). In other words, *glory is the ultimate meaning of our suffering.* And glory will not come any other way. Jesus was resurrected but not before his death. This is why in Mark's Gospel three times we see Jesus teaching his disciples about the necessary road to Calvary that would precede his resurrection (8:31; 9:30–31; 10:33–34). There was an exaltation but not apart from the humiliation of the cross. This is Paul's point in Philippians 2:5–11:

> Have this mind among yourselves, which is yours in Christ Jesus, who, though he was in the form of God, did not count equality with God a thing to be grasped, but emptied himself, by taking the form of a servant, being born in the likeness of men. And being found in human form, he humbled himself by becoming obedient to the point of death, even death on a cross. Therefore God has highly exalted him and bestowed on him the name that is above every name, so that at the name of Jesus every knee should bow, in heaven and on earth and under the earth, and every tongue confess that Jesus Christ is Lord, to the glory of God the Father.

Paul makes it clear that this pattern of humiliation to exaltation is the Christian's pattern when he exhorts us to "Have this mind among yourselves" (v. 5). Paul knows that he must "share Christ's sufferings" if he would "attain the resurrection from the dead" (3:10). And according to the design of God, "this light momentary affliction is preparing for us an eternal weight of glory beyond all comparison" (2 Cor 4:17). As Murray Harris comments on this verse, "In the divine economy, affliction actually generates glory."[16] Disciples of Christ must "follow in his steps" (1 Pet 2:21).

---

16 Murray J. Harris, *The Second Epistle to the Corinthians*, NIGTC (Eerdmans, 2005), 362. See also George H. Guthrie, who writes, "The verb κατεργαζομαι (*katergazomai*), which Paul uses extensively, has to do with accomplishing or producing something, or bringing something about." George H. Guthrie, *2 Corinthians*, BECNT (Baker Academic, 2015), 271–272. Or as Mark Seifrid explains, "Present suffering and affliction is thus not vain and pointless. To the contrary, in God's hand it works an 'eternal weight of glory' beyond all measure." Mark Seifrid, *The Second Letter to the Corinthians*, PNTC (Eerdmans, 2014), 218.

And those steps take the Christian "outside the camp" to "bear the reproach he endured" (Heb 13:13).

Of course, none of this should surprise the student of the Bible for it was Jesus himself who explained the essence of discipleship when he said, "If anyone would come after me, let him deny himself and take up his cross and follow me" (Mark 8:34). The prosperity gospel knows nothing of denying self or of taking up a cross. After all, what is a cross but an emblem of suffering and shame? Prosperity preachers peddle a "gospel" of self-indulgence and ease, a message that misses the design of God in salvation. In one form or another, they teach that suffering and affliction are inconsistent with the victorious life Jesus wants them to have.

The Geneva Reformer John Calvin explains the design of God in the Christian's suffering when he comments on Romans 8:17: "Various are the interpretations of this passage, but I approve of the following in preference to any other, 'We are co-heirs with Christ, provided, in entering our inheritance, we follow him in the same way in which he has gone before.'" And what is the way of Christ, according to Calvin? "Christ came to it [his inheritance] by the cross; then we must come to it in the same manner."[17] Likewise, Charles Hodge, the nineteenth-century Princeton divine, saw the necessary connection between the Christian's suffering and final salvation:

> We suffer as Christ suffered, not only when we are subject to the contradiction of sinners, but in the ordinary sorrows of life in which he, the man of sorrows, so largely shared. We are said to suffer with Christ ἵνα, "in order that," we may be glorified together. That is, the design of God in the affliction of his people, is not to satisfy the demands of justice, but to prepare them to participate in his glory. To creatures in a state of sin, suffering is the necessary condition of exaltation.[18]

More recently, Leon Morris notes how the Christian's suffering on

---

17 John Calvin, *Commentaries on the Epistle of Paul the Apostle to the Romans* (1539; repr., Baker, 2009), 301–302.

18 Charles Hodge, *Romans*, Geneva Commentary Series (1835; repr., Banner of Truth Trust, 1989), 268.

the way to glory is "not some perverse accident." He explains, "Neither Paul nor any other New Testament writer lets us forget that believers have no easy path. Their Master suffered, and they are called to suffer, too. This is not some perverse accident but an integral part of discipleship .... [O]ur sufferings are not meaningless. We suffer *in order that we may also share in his glory*. The path of suffering is the path to glory."[19] Perhaps Douglas Moo summarizes this teaching best when he states,

> Because we are one with Christ, we are his fellow heirs, assured of being "glorified with him." But, at the same time, this oneness means that we must follow Christ's own road to glory, "suffering with him" .... [T]he suffering Paul speaks of here refers to the daily anxieties, tensions, and persecutions that are the lot of those who follow the one who was "reckoned with the transgressors" (Luke 22:37). Paul makes clear that this suffering is the condition for the inheritance; we will be "glorified with" Christ (only) *if* we "suffer with him." Participation in Christ's glory can come only through participation in his suffering. What Paul is doing is setting forth an unbreakable "law of the kingdom" according to which glory can come only by way of suffering.[20]

The great tragedy of the prosperity gospel is that it teaches a way to glory contrary to God's design. Like Formalist and Hypocrisy in *The Pilgrim's Progress* who thought they could bypass the Kingsway and blaze a trail of their own, prosperity preachers announce a way to glory that, in the end, leads only to destruction.

Implications for Pastoral Ministry

The implications of this teaching for pastoral ministry are

---

19 Leon Morris, *The Epistle to the Romans* (Eerdmans, 1995), 318, italics original.

20 Douglas J. Moo, *The Epistle to the Romans*, NICNT (Eerdmans, 1996), 505–506. See also John Murray, who states, "There is no sharing in Christ's glory unless there is sharing in his sufferings." John Murray, *The Epistle to the Romans* (1959; repr., Eerdmans, 1997), 299.

significant. A Pauline theology of suffering as outlined above means that churches need not prosperity pastors but pilgrim pastors. In contrast to the prosperity pastor, a pilgrim pastor assumes that pastors and their people will suffer. Indeed, because God has ordained suffering as the way to glory a pastor *thinks* a particular way about ministry. In this section, I outline the hallmarks of a prosperity pastor and a pilgrim pastor commending the latter for our churches today.

Prosperity Pastors

Prosperity pastors are not new. And they have their roots in soil much older than the ministry of E. W. Kenyon, the late nineteenth-century, early twentieth-century evangelist whose "positive confession" theology helped birth Word of Faith Pentecostalism.[21] In fact, we see prosperity pastors in Ezekiel 34:1–6:

> The word of the Lord came to me: "Son of man, prophesy against the shepherds of Israel; prophesy, and say to them, even to the shepherds, Thus says the Lord God: Ah, shepherds of Israel who have been feeding yourselves! Should not shepherds feed the sheep? You eat the fat, you clothe yourselves with the wool, you slaughter the fat ones, but you do not feed the sheep. The weak you have not strengthened, the sick you have not healed, the injured you have not bound up, the strayed you have not brought back, the lost you have not sought, and with force and harshness you have ruled them. So they were scattered, because there was no shepherd, and they became food for all the wild beasts. My sheep were scattered; they wandered over all the mountains and on every high hill. My sheep were scattered over all the face of the earth, with none to search or seek for them." (cf. Jer 23:1–4)

The metaphor of "shepherd" is being used to describe the leaders of Judah. Clearly, these shepherds are benefiting at great cost to the

---

21 For a helpful discussion of Kenyon's ministry and his role in the history of the prosperity gospel, see Bowler, *Blessed*, 15–20.

sheep. They are abusing their power by lording it over the people for their own selfish gain. Like contemporary prosperity pastors, these corrupt shepherds are using people to satisfy their own appetites for power and riches. The indictment is severe: "You eat the fat, you clothe yourselves with the wool, you slaughter the fat ones, but you do not feed the sheep" (v. 3). The consequences for the people are tragic. Those who remain under this tyranny are resigned to perish in gross neglect, while other sheep are scattered and lost, left to "become food for all the wild beasts" (v. 5).

Of course, God will not allow this to go on forever. After rehearsing his indictment on the faithless shepherds, God announces the judgement: "Thus says the Lord GOD, Behold, I am against the shepherds, and I will require my sheep at their hand and put a stop to their feeding the sheep. No longer shall the shepherds feed themselves. I will rescue my sheep from their mouths, that they may not be food for them" (v. 10). The Lord declares that he is "against the shepherds," a posture he undoubtedly has toward contemporary prosperity pastors.

Pilgrim Pastors

Pilgrim pastors, unlike prosperity pastors, take seriously the example of Jesus who "set his face to go to Jerusalem" (Luke 9:51; cf. Isa 50:7). Pilgrim pastors are theologians of the cross who seek to embody the sacrifice of Christ in the service of his people (Col 1:24). After all, it was Jesus who set himself apart from the faithless shepherds of Ezekiel 34 when he said, "I am the good shepherd. The good shepherd lays down his life for the sheep" (John 10:11). Our suffering, of course, is not at all redemptive or atoning like that of Jesus. As Michael Horton explains, "His suffering was redemptive, whereas ours is a participation in that already accomplished victory. But our cross-bearing is still real. It is not another cross that we bear, our own burden for sin and guilt, but sharing in his humiliation and shame as those who belong to him."[22] This is why ministry for pilgrim pastors is not about using people as a means to the end

---

22 Michael Horton, *A Place for Weakness: Preparing Yourself for Suffering* (Zondervan, 2006), 47.

of their wealth or platform or influence or fame, but a laying down of their lives for the good of the churches they serve.

In Mark's Gospel, we see two prosperity pastors in training—that is, until Jesus takes hold of the curriculum. This familiar story features James and John in the grip of a theology of glory as they approach Jesus with an audacious request: "And James and John, the sons of Zebedee, came up to him and said to him, 'Teacher, we want you to do for us whatever we ask of you.' And he said to them, 'What do you want me to do for you?' And they said to him, 'Grant us to sit, one at your right hand and one at your left, in your glory'" (Mark 10:35–37). James and John *thought* they knew what Jesus's ministry was all about: a theology of glory that would have him sitting in the halls of power once his military and political kingdom was established in Jerusalem. And they wanted in. Sensing this, Jesus begins to set them straight about the heart of his mission and what would be the implications for them:

> Jesus said to them, "You do not know what you are asking. Are you able to drink the cup that I drink, or to be baptized with the baptism with which I am baptized?" And they said to him, "We are able." And Jesus said to them, "The cup that I drink you will drink, and with the baptism with which I am baptized, you will be baptized, but to sit at my right hand or at my left is not mine to grant, but it is for those for whom it has been prepared." (vv. 38–40)

What do the images of "cup" and "baptism" signify for Jesus? Jesus recognizes that his messianic mission is to drink the *cup* of God's wrath for sin and suffer under the *baptism* of God's judgment on sin (cf. Mark 14:36; Luke 12:50). How do these images of "cup" and "baptism" apply to the disciples? Not in a judicial sense, but in a moral sense. This imagery refers to the persecutions and sufferings that will inevitably fall upon those who follow Christ in salvation. In other words, this is a reminder that sacrifice and suffering is the way of Jesus and, therefore, the path of all who would follow him.

This story continues with particular application to those who would be leaders in the church. Jesus proceeds to give foundational training in being a pilgrim pastor:

> And when the ten heard it, they began to be indignant at James and John. And Jesus called them to him and said to them, "You know that those who are considered rulers of the Gentiles lord it over them, and their great ones exercise authority over them. But it shall not be so among you. But whoever would be great among you must be your servant, and whoever would be first among you must be slave of all. For even the Son of Man came not to be served but to serve, and to give his life as a ransom for many." (Mark 10:41–45)

Servants and slaves. This is the outcome of those who understand that suffering is the way of Christ. After all, "*even* the Son of Man came not to be served but to serve, and to give his life as a ransom for many" (v. 45, italics added). A pastor's leadership in the church is governed by his fellowship in the sufferings of Christ.

Rethinking Seminary Training

As a seminary professor, I am concerned with what I hear from some of my students about their desires for ministry. Too often the "vision" for ministry sounds more "prosperity" than "pilgrim." The causes for this, I imagine, are manifold, and the seminaries are not entirely to blame. But those of us entrusted with the vital work of theological education would do well to examine our curriculum and manner of teaching. A series of questions come to mind:

1. Does our *curriculum*, as evidenced in our lectures and syllabi (particularly in our systematic theology, pastoral theology, and leadership disciplines), emphasize a Pauline theology of suffering?
2. Does the *manner* of our teaching embody something of what it means to "take up our cross and follow him?" In other words, are we communicating with an urgency and soberness in accordance with what we know to be true about the way to glory?

3. Are we thinking critically and deeply about how a Pauline theology of suffering translates to *online education*? How should a robustly biblical anthropology inform our pedagogy in our digital age?
4. As more seminaries are partnering with other institutions to offer an MBA alongside an MDiv, what are we doing to ensure that we are training not corporate executives, but *pastor-theologians* for the church?
5. Are *we* pilgrim professors as evidenced by our life and doctrine?

How we answer these questions will help determine what kind of leaders our seminaries are producing. With secularization continuing to spread throughout the Western world with the paradoxical rise in the challenge of Islam, our seminaries must be vigorous training grounds in sound doctrine and true piety. Indeed, the greatest need of our churches is pilgrim pastors. Our seminaries have the human capital and physical resources to serve as the premier institutions for this vital work. The question is, do we have the vision and the will to do so?

Conclusion

In this chapter, I argued that the prosperity gospel is inconsistent with a Pauline theology of suffering, and therefore, what the prosperity gospel offers is no gospel at all. As demonstrated, suffering is the way to glory and glory is the ultimate meaning of our suffering. Like Formalist and Hypocrisy in Bunyan's classic, the prosperity gospel seeks its own way to glory rather than obedience to the Kingsway. Tragically, the end of the path of prosperity teaching is destruction; nothing less than eternity is at stake. For this reason, and for the sake of pilgrim pastors in our day, a Pauline theology of suffering is essential to reclaim and propagate.

4

The Unique Temptations of Wealth and Poverty Over Time

David S. Kotter

Introduction

THE PSALMIST SANG OUT, "Hear this, all peoples! Give ear, all inhabitants of the world, both low and high, rich and poor together!" (Ps 49:1–2).[1] In this statement, the author implicitly recognized two different groups of people based on economic status. Similar to the Psalmist, Paul distinguished between men and women (1 Tim 2:8–10) and young and old (Titus 2:2–6) as distinct groups having unique characteristics, responsibilities, and temptations. Likewise, both Jews and Gentiles as well as slave and free (Gal 3:28) share a common identity in Christ while retaining distinctions between groups.

The physical distinctions between men and women, young and old remain largely the same since the first century. On the other hand, the difference between slave and free has been substantially removed over the past two centuries, though tragically slavery of various sorts persists in some places. In contrast, the disparity between rich and poor has dramatically widened over the time since the industrial revolution. Fortunately, the poor around the world have grown wealthier on average, while the rich have multiplied riches even faster.

This chapter intends to examine the biblical admonitions to both the rich and the poor to identify the unique temptations faced by each group, then to use an interdisciplinary economic approach to analyze how these temptations have changed from the

---

1 Unless otherwise noted, all Scripture quotations come from the ESV.

first-century culture surrounding the New Testament to the present day (where Big Data has compounded the effects of the Industrial Revolution). This chapter seeks to support the church by highlighting the changes in the types and intensity of temptations posed by economic growth over time and also by encouraging further research in this critical and fruitful area.

The Barna Group documented such trends in a 2013 study on the changing shape of temptations between different groups of people over the last few decades.[2] David Kinnaman, president of Barna Group, remarked that temptation had gone virtual and affected millennials in significantly different ways than "elders."[3] Notably, 25 percent of millennials confessed to expressing anger or "going off" on someone via text or email, while only 5 percent of elders confided in experiencing this type of temptation to wrath. Likewise, 37 percent of millennials as opposed to 13 percent of elders confessed to gossiping because of the ability to express oneself digitally on social media.

If the Barna research demonstrates changes in temptations over decades, then it is likely that economic and information shifts over centuries have also produced changes in the types of temptations faced by individual Christians. For example, the ability to obey the command in Ephesians 4:28 to not steal but rather to work quietly might have changed little over time. On the other hand, the admonition not to covet or envy (Exod 20:17; Rom 7:7) possibly has grown more difficult with the proliferation of digital media displaying the bodies and lifestyles of the very rich. Likewise, the vast increase in worldwide wealth should make it easier to be generous compared with the first-century world (1 Tim 6:18–19; 2 Cor 9:11). Yet the temptation to flaunt wealth (1 Tim 2:9; 1 Pet 3:3–4; cf. Jas 2:2) probably has grown with the proliferation of options to display luxury for others to see, especially on social media platforms. The imperative to be content in all circumstances (Heb 13:5; cf. 1 Tim

---

2 Todd Hunter, "New Research Explores the Changing Shape of Temptation," Barna Group, 25 January 2013, https://www.barna.com/research/new-research-explores-the-changing-shape-of-temptation/.

3 In the Barna study, "elders" were classified as people born before 1945 and "millennials" as people born between 1984 and 2002. Hunter, "New Research Explores Temptation."

6:8; Phil 4:11) should be easier today in an absolute sense with the greater availability of food and clothing. Unfortunately, the propensity of most people to adopt a relative standard of poverty (a comparison with other people) rather than an absolute standard (considering only what a human being needs to survive) suggests that the temptation to discontent probably has grown worse.

In summary, although the ethical requirements of the Bible remain timeless, the changes in culture over time affect the relative challenges to obedience as Christians. This cross-disciplinary analysis of changes in temptations will begin with a review of average changes in poverty and wealth since the time of the New Testament along with a brief consideration of the explosive growth in social media. With this foundation established, three examples of the unique temptations of the poor will be considered followed by a similar examination of shifts in three cases of temptations of the rich. The chapter will conclude with recommendations for the church and thoughts about further areas of research and investigation.

Selected Economic Changes Since the Time of the New Testament

A survey of economic changes over the past two millennia has already filled many books, but this section briefly establishes a basis for this evaluation of temptations of the rich and poor with a review of the trends in extreme poverty, average individual income, and household wealth. The investigation will focus on the United States, which provides more precise economic data, yet worldwide data will be provided to the extent that it is available. After the economic summary, a brief overview of the astronomical growth of social media for the past two decades will be evaluated as a basis for variations in the nature and intensity of temptations unique to the rich and poor.

Downward Trends of Poverty

The World Bank has defined the international extreme poverty level as $1.90 per person per day in 2011 dollars.⁴ Applying this standard to the first century implies that during the time of the New Testament more than 82 percent of people lived in poverty.⁵ The proportion of the population living in poverty remained at about 80 percent all the way up to 1800 at the outset of the Industrial Revolution.⁶ Half the world (50 percent) lived in poverty in 1966, and according to the World Bank, this percentage had declined dramatically to 9 percent by 2019. While the trend is extremely encouraging, the absolute number of 689 million people persisting in poverty remains a tragedy. In the United States, the Census Bureau defines poverty relative to the size of the family and age of the members.⁷ Using this reckoning, 10.5 percent of the population lived below the poverty line of $26,200 per year for a family of four in 2020.⁸

Applying these facts to the New Testament, when Paul was admonished by the church in Jerusalem to remember the poor (the very thing he was eager to do; Gal 2:10), more than 80 percent of the people were poor, while today about 90 percent of people live above a more generous measure of poverty. For Christians to remember the 10 percent who are poor (either by worldwide or United States standards) seems to be an entirely different proposition than what existed during Paul's time. It would seem reasonable to expect that the unique temptations faced by the poor have changed over time.

---

4 World Bank, "Global Poverty Line Update," 30 September 2015, https://www.worldbank.org/en/topic/poverty/brief/global-poverty-line-faq.

5 Longenecker estimates that 55 percent of people were living at or below subsistence level. An additional 27 percent were living at subsistence or had a surplus sufficient for survival. Bruce W. Longenecker, *Remember the Poor: Paul, Poverty, and the Greco-Roman World* (Eerdmans, 2010), 53.

6 Gapminder, "Extreme Poverty Trend," accessed 24 November 2021, https://www.gapminder.org/topics/extreme-poverty-trend.

7 United States Census Bureau, "How the Census Bureau Measures Poverty," 22 November 2021, https://www.census.gov/topics/income-poverty/poverty/guidance/poverty-measures.html.

8 Sevil Omer, "Global Poverty: Facts, FAQs, and How to Help," World Vision, 23 August 2021, https://www.worldvision.org/sponsorship-news-stories/global-poverty-facts.

Upward Trends of Personal Income and Wealth

While the downward trend of people living in poverty is important, the picture is even more dramatic when considering increases in individual income over the centuries. In the United States, personal income can be estimated using Gross Domestic Product (GDP) per capita. This measure of all the goods and services produced in the United States in a given year divided by the number of residents provides a rough measure of wages or income per person. In 1960, individual income averaged $3,007 in the United States, and this figure increased more than 20 times to $65,280 by 2019.[9] On a worldwide basis, average income in 1960 was $445 per person or $1.22 per day, which is consistent with the data that the average person around the world lived in abject poverty. Income per person around the world increased more than 25 times to $11,417 per person in 2019, which is a faster rate of growth than the United States over the same period.[10]

These trends of increasing wealth are averages which obscure the fact that the rate of increase for the very rich has been even higher. This reality can be illuminated by examining the percentage of total wealth in the United States controlled by the very rich. The National Bureau of Economic Research reports that in 1962 the top 5 percent of households controlled 54 percent of all the wealth in the United States, but by 2019, the top 5 percent controlled 66 percent of all the wealth. While the poor have moved away from subsistence and have been growing in wealth over the past 60 years, the rich have been getting richer at an even faster pace.[11] Accordingly, the number of millionaires in the United States (in constant 1995 dollars adjusted for inflation) nearly quadrupled from 2.4 million in 1983 to 9.3 million in 2019.

---

9 Macrotrends, "U.S. GDP Per Capita 1960–2021," accessed 24 November 2021, https://www.macrotrends.net/countries/USA/united-states/gdp-per-capita.

10 Macrotrends, "U.S. GDP Per Capita 1960–2021."

11 Edward N. Wolff, "Household Wealth Trends in the United States, 1962 to 2019: Median Wealth Rebounds... But Not Enough," NBER Working Papers Series (National Bureau of Economic Research, 2021), 49, https://www.nber.org/system/files/working_papers/w28383/w28383.pdf.

A thorough discussion of the ethics and economic implications of this increase in financial inequality is beyond the scope of this chapter. Nevertheless, for the sake of this study, these trends demonstrate that the number of people facing the unique temptations of the rich has been increasing over the past four decades and that the focus of the biblical teaching of the church should adjust along with this changing trend. Though the ethical requirements of the Bible are timeless, it will be profitable to consider how the nature and intensity of these temptations have changed as a result of such consequential economic shifts.

Unprecedented Changes in Personal Communication

The decline in poverty and dramatic increase in wealth are not the only spiritually relevant aspects of culture that have changed. The ability to communicate personally with billions of people seemed impossible until the past few decades. Further, the ability to privately observe the lives of millions of people was simply inconceivable until the twenty-first century. The advent and astonishing growth of social media have intensified temptations that were humanly unforeseen when the New Testament was written.

For example, YouTube began in Menlo Park, California on February 14, 2005, with an 18 second video of Jawed Karim entitled "Me at the Zoo" that featured him standing in front of elephants at the San Diego Zoo. By October of that year, a single video featuring a soccer player with Nike shoes reached 1 million views for the first time. YouTube was acquired by Google 18 months later, and the "Evolution of Dance" hit 100 million views in 2008. In 2009 YouTube reached 1 billion views per day in total, and by 2012 "Gangnam Style" first reached 1 billion views of a single video.[12] In the same year, YouTube earned $14 billion in ad revenue based on an average of 1 billion videos viewed every single day.[13] By 2021, YouTube had 5 billion views per day of 26 billion unique

---

12 Paige Leskin, "YouTube Is 15 Years Old," *Business Insider*, 30 May 30 2020, https://www.businessinsider.com/history-of-youtube-in-photos-2015-10.

13 Kit Smith, "57 Fascinating and Incredible YouTube Statistics," Brandwatch, 21 February 2020, https://www.brandwatch.com/blog/youtube-stats.

uploaded videos. These statistics represent only one of many video sharing platforms, and the worldwide count could be expanded exponentially by considering Vimeo, Panopto, Brightcove, Kaltura, Qumu, and more.[14]

Likewise, Facebook (now part of Meta Platforms, Inc. as of October 29, 2021) was founded in 2004 in Cambridge, Massachusetts, and was opened to the world in September 2006. Since that time, unrelenting growth reached 2.9 billion users by July 2021. This user base overlaps somewhat with the more than one billion users of Instagram and two billion active users of WhatsApp who send more than a 100 billion messages every day. Adding Asian apps such as WeChat, Weibo, TikTok, and Tencent reaches a majority of the population of the planet and places more information in the palm of one's hand than ever before in history. Mark Zuckerberg's plans for a "Metaverse" intends to make a further quantum leap of social media into every aspect of life.[15]

In summary, economic forces have fundamentally changed the way that people live and have an impact on the spiritual life of individuals as well, specifically in presenting different types and intensities of temptation than ever before. In the same way, the extent of social media and the access to information strengthens certain temptations in ways that have never been experienced in the church before this generation.

Illustrations of the Spiritual Effects of Economic and Media Trends

Before proceeding further, two illustrations might make these changes more concrete. Historically, one of the primary ways for landowners to help the poor was to provide food according to the gleaning laws. These laws stated, "When you reap the harvest of your land, you shall not reap your field right up to its edge, nor

---

14 Panopto, "Comparing the Top Online Video Platforms," 15 February 2021, https://www.panopto.com/blog/comparing-the-top-online-video-platforms.

15 Mark Zuckerberg, "Connect 2021: Our Vision for the Metaverse," Facebook, 28 October 2021, https://www.facebook.com/4/videos/connect-2021-our-vision-for-the-metaverse/1898414763675286.

shall you gather the gleanings after your harvest. You shall leave them for the poor and for the sojourner: I am the LORD your God" (Lev 19:9–10). The efficacy of these laws was famously illustrated in the book of Ruth (2:2–15), and they ended up serving the poor through the many centuries of essentially unchanged agricultural practices. Unfortunately, the advent of modern agribusiness in the United States over the past 30 years means poor people in urban settings no longer can benefit from gleaning in fields. Specifically, just under 40 percent of the total population lived on farms in the United States in 1900 and about 60 percent lived in rural areas with access to farmlands.[16] Since that time, the average farm size tripled from about 150 acres to almost 450 acres, and the productivity of crops produced per acre has increased fivefold.[17] These trends mean that most poor people neither have access to the tiny percentage of crops left in fields nor the ability to grind flour for baking bread. While the biblical principle of helping the poor remains the same, evidently the means must change along with these positive economic and technological advances.

The second illustration of how economic changes require a rethinking of direct biblical commands can be found in the teachings of John the Baptist. When the crowds along the Jordan River were cut to the heart (after being called a brood of vipers), they asked John the Baptist, "What then shall we do?" (Luke 3:10). His response was direct: "Whoever has two tunics is to share with him who has none, and whoever has food is to do likewise" (Luke 3:11). If a preacher in the United States in the twenty-first century was to deliver such an admonition, it is possible that his congregation would erupt in laughter. Even the most sacrificial and generous Christians could at least fill a suitcase with garments, and the average believer in the United States almost certainly has a closet bulging with clothes. The invention of synthetic fibers means

---

16 Jayson Lusk, "The Evolution of American Agriculture," Jayson Lusk (blog), 27 June 2016, http://jaysonlusk.com/blog/2016/6/26/the-evolution-of-american-agriculture.

17 Jody McDaniel and Bruce Boess, "Farms and Land in Farms 2019 Summary" (USDA National Agricultural Statistics Service, 2020), 1–17, https://downloads.usda.library.cornell.edu/usda-esmis/files/5712m6524/k0698r168/2b88qx13z/fnlo0220.pdf.

that clothing simply does not wear out as fast as it did in the first century. Therefore, few homeless people lack clothes because inexpensive clothing is available at second-hand shops or the Salvation Army. Though the principle of generosity remains unchanged, this example raises the question as to a Christian's obligations when clothing is abundantly available.

This section illustrated how cultural changes require the church to revisit the timeless teachings of the Bible to better apply the principles to the current situation. The next two sections consider the unique temptations faced by the poor and the rich, and how the growth of social media and economic advancement have changed the nature of temptation.

Unique Temptations of the Poor

Not only the Psalmist in the Bible but also James and John recognize categorical differences between the lives of the rich and poor (Jas 2:1–7; Rev 6:15–17). This section does not have sufficient space to examine all of the issues of poor people but will consider three representative temptations that have changed along with economic advancement and social media reach: gluttony, covetousness, and sloth.

Gluttony

Gluttony might seem like an unusual place to begin in an analysis of changes in temptation over time, especially since few churches actually discuss the temptation toward gluttony. Nevertheless, gluttony is relevant since it historically has been classified as one of the seven deadly sins or iniquities that tend to lead to further acts of iniquity. Further, gluttony is one of the most straightforward temptations to document with changes through time.

Whether or not it is taught in local churches, the Bible is clearly opposed to gluttony. Young men are warned to "be not among drunkards or among gluttonous eaters of meat, for the drunkard and the glutton will come to poverty" (Prov 23:20–21). Even a companion of gluttons is shameful to his parents (Prov 28:7). This is not an admonition against all feasting, since feasts are encouraged in the Pentateuch (cf. Exod 23:14; Deut 12:7; 14:23–26). Jesus himself attended feasts where he was (erroneously) accused of being a glutton (Matt 11:19).

Although the temptation toward gluttony has always been in the human heart, the means to be gluttonous is a relatively recent phenomenon. The increase in average worldwide income has been documented in the first section of this chapter. While the sticker prices of food may seem nominally high and the year 2021 has seen a surge in food inflationary pressures, the absolute cost of food has never been lower.[18] In 1913, the average worker had to labor 3 ½ hours to purchase a chicken, while in 2013, the cost of a chicken measured in work time had fallen to about seven minutes.[19] Measuring the cost in human effort avoids inflationary distortions and shows that the real cost of a standard frying chicken has fallen 96 percent over the past century.

Consistent with these dramatic decreases in real prices, the 2013 Barna study of changes in temptations reported that 62 percent of baby boomers (people born between 1946 and 1964) confessed to eating too much. This is a remarkable statistic, especially in light of the fact that historically the vast majority of people were at greater risk of starvation than overeating. In other words, economic developments have presented the majority of people in the United States not only with the temptation of television channels exclusively devoted to preparing food but also the means to actually carry out the sin of gluttony.

Further evidence that the temptation and ability to commit the sin of gluttony is greater than ever before in history can be seen in the rates of obesity in the United States and around the world. One quarter of veterans measured by body mass index (BMI) in 1870 were found to be overweight, but by 1976, about 47 percent

---

18 Samantha Pearson and Luciana Magalhaes, "Global Food Prices Surge as Inflation Spreads," *Wall Street Journal*, 5 November 2021, https://www.wsj.com/articles/global-food-prices-surge-as-inflation-spreads-11636119367.

19 David Kotter, "Working for the Glory of God: The Distinction between Greed and Self-Interest in the Life and Letters of the Apostle Paul" (PhD diss., The Southern Baptist Theological Seminary, 2015), 104.

of Americans were overweight.[20] The US Center for Disease Control (CDC) reported in 2010 that three quarters (75.4 percent) of adults were overweight, obese, or extremely obese.[21] While gaining weight can have many causes, such broad trends across a population of over 330 million people suggest that people are not only tempted to gluttony but that they are succumbing to the sin at rates never before seen in history.

Covetousness

A second changing temptation is toward covetousness. God's position on coveting is comprehensive in the tenth commandment, "You shall not covet your neighbor's house; you shall not covet your neighbor's wife, or his male servant, or his female servant, or his ox, or his donkey, or anything that is your neighbor's" (Exod 20:17). Likewise, the prophet Micah condemned oppressors who coveted the fields of others (Mic 2:2), and Jesus denounced coveting in a laundry list of evil that proceeds from within the heart (Mark 7:20–23; cf. Luke 12:15).

In the Roman Empire, the vast majority of people rarely had the opportunity to travel beyond a local village. The opportunities for coveting were limited to what could be seen nearby or to tales of riches related from far away. In the twenty-first century, riches are not only displayed in person but also through social media on the web. The 2013 Barna study reported that 41 percent of the digital-native millennials confessed to being envious of others while only 13 percent of elders reported the same temptation.[22] This data suggests that the temptation toward covetousness is stronger than during the time of the New Testament.

---

20 David Kotter, "Eat and Be Content: The Gospel Solution to Our Eating Problems" (address given to the Seminary Wives Institute at The Southern Baptist Theological Seminary, Louisville, KY, 1 October 2013), 19.

21 Cheryl D. Fryar, Margaret D. Carroll, and Cynthia L. Ogden, "Prevalence of Overweight, Obesity, and Extreme Obesity Among Adults: United States Trends 1960–1962 through 2009–2010," CDC National Center for Health Statistics, 6 November 2015, https://www.cdc.gov/nchs/data/hestat/obesity_adult_09_10/obesity_adult_09_10.htm.

22 Hunter, "New Research Explores Temptation."

Further, the unveiling of internal records from Facebook by the *Wall Street Journal* supports this assertion, especially that employees recognized that the Instagram platform made body image issues worse for one in three teen girls.[23] This effect was especially true concerning "so-called social comparison, which is when people assess their own value in relation to the attractiveness, wealth, and success of others."[24] From the internal Facebook files, the *Wall Street Journal* reported, "The tendency to share only the best moments, a pressure to look perfect and an addictive product can send teens spiraling toward eating disorders, an unhealthy sense of their own bodies, and depression."[25]

The average size of a medieval village generally was between 50 and 100 people, and everybody likely was familiar with every one of the residents.[26] In such a context, repeated over and over across the countryside, it was possible to be considered the prettiest girl in the village. Now every teenage girl competes with the very best in the world for attention, and this has dramatically increased the temptation toward envy and covetousness.

Sloth

A third temptation for the poor that has changed with economic growth over time is the temptation toward sloth. Historically, hunger was the driver for most laborers. Proverbs 16:26 states, "The appetite of laborers works for them; their hunger drives them on"

---

[23] Georgia Wells, Jeff Horwitz, and Deepa Seetharaman, "Facebook Knows Instagram Is Toxic for Teen Girls, Company Documents Show," *Wall Street Journal*, 14 September 2021, https://www.wsj.com/articles/facebook-knows-instagram-is-toxic-for-teen-girls-company-documents-show-11631620739?mod=Searchresults_pos20&page=1.

[24] The *Wall Street Journal* reports from internal Facebook documents that social comparison is worse on Instagram which focuses more heavily on body image and lifestyle than other platforms such as TikTok or Snapchat. In other words, the features identified as most harmful to teens are at the core of the Instagram platform. Wells, Horwitz, and Seetharaman, "Facebook Knows Instagram Is Toxic for Teen Girls, Company Documents Show"

[25] Wells, Horwitz, and Seetharaman, "Facebook Knows Instagram Is Toxic."

[26] Medieval Chronicles, "Medieval Village," accessed 24 November 2021, https://www.medievalchronicles.com/medieval-life/medieval-village.

(NIV). While it is difficult to measure hunger related to work on an individual basis, more broadly the rates of death by famine in the world have declined from 142 per 100,000 in the decade of the 1870's to 0.5 per 100,000 in the years between 2010 and 2016.[27] The most recent figures would be even lower except for wars and communist policies which created artificial famines.[28]

The United States has not experienced a famine in the past century, so in 1995, the United States Department of Agriculture (USDA) has conducted household surveys of "food security."[29] According to these statistics, 4 percent of households in the United States self-reported low food security in 2019. Compared to worldwide history, having more than 96 percent of the population with regular access to nutritional foods is without precedent. In other words, the motivation toward work because of hunger has never been lower.

Another indirect measure of the temptation toward sloth based on data from the United States would be the employment index which broadly divides the number of people with jobs by the total population. In April 2000, the US employment rate was 65 percent, and this has declined to 51 percent in 2020.[30] Without other significant changes in the total population, this data suggests that

---

27 Marta Schoch and Christoph Lakner, "Global Poverty Reduction Is Slowing," World Bank Blogs, 5 November 2020, https://blogs.worldbank.org/opendata/global-poverty-reduction-slowing-regional-trends-help-understanding-why.

28 Sadly, of the top ten famines ranked by excess mortality as a proportion of the population, six of them were in Socialist countries (Cambodia, Ukrainian SSR, North Korea, Soviet Union, China, and Ethiopia, in order of severity). Three were caused by civil wars or genocide (Rwanda, Somalia, and Nigeria) and only one by poverty exacerbated by a natural disaster (Bangladesh). Our World in Data, "Long Term Trends in Global Famine Mortality," accessed 24 November 2021, https://ourworldindata.org/famines#long-term-trends-in-global-famine-mortality.

29 Under the USDA definition, "Very Low Food Security" is neither starvation nor necessarily even hunger, but rather "reports of multiple indications of disrupted eating patterns and reduced food intake." Alisha Coleman-Jensen, Matthew P. Rabbitt, Laura Hales, and Christian A. Gregory, "Definitions of Food Security," USDA Economic Research Service, last modified 8 September 2021, https://www.ers.usda.gov/topics/food-nutrition-assistance/food-security-in-the-us/definitions-of-food-security.aspx.

30 Trading Economics, "United States Employment Rate," accessed 24 November 2021, https://tradingeconomics.com/united-states/employment-rate.

one out of every five people employed in 2000 had either retired, become disabled, or otherwise left paid employment.[31]

The declining cost of food and significant increase in safety nets has intensified this temptation for many.[32] Predictably, demands have escalated for a Universal Basic Income (UBI) involving payments of up to $1,200 per month per person over 21 years old without any requirement of need or ability to work. Unfortunately, experience with the supplemental employment benefits during the COVID-19 pandemic suggests that universal payments or even increased child income tax credits likely has a material effect in causing declines in the desire to seek paid employment.

Of course, some people might not be recorded in these employment statistics because of a preference for nonpaid occupations such as community volunteers or serving in churches. Even so, no population in history could ever feed and provide for every member (including the elderly and children) with only 51 percent of the people employed, and this is consistent with a downward trend in hunger as a motivation for work. While the temptation to sloth has always been present, few people in the ancient world could afford the choice to be lazy and not work diligently in order to avoid starvation. Not surprisingly, the 2013 Barna study reports that 56 percent of millennial's confessed to being lazy or not working as hard as one should compared to 30 percent of the elders polled in the research.[33]

---

31 A more precise statistic to measure this phenomenon would be the labor force participation rate, which only considers people 16 years and over who have jobs of any type or are looking for employment. Nevertheless, the trend is consistent as the labor force participation rate declined from 67 percent in 2002 to 61 percent in 2020. This more precise figure eliminates the consideration of changes in total population such as changes in the proportion of children. Trading Economics, "Unites States Labor Force Participation Rate," accessed 24 November 2021, https://tradingeconomics.com/united-states/labor-force-participation-rate.

32 Ben Carson, "America Needs a Safety Net, Not a Hammock," *Wall Street Journal*, 5 November 2021, https://www.wsj.com/articles/america-safety-net-entitlements-work-requirements-donations-build-back-better-biden-charity-11636123429?mod=Searchresults_pos1&page=1.

33 Hunter, "New Research Explores Temptation."

Unique Temptations of the Rich

The same sins can exist in the human heart whether one is rich or poor, but economic advantages provide the ability to physically express sinful desires that are not available to the poor. As before, this section does not have sufficient space to examine all of the temptations that likely have increased for rich people but will consider three representative examples: pridefully keeping up appearances, trusting in riches, and finding satisfaction in riches as a form of idolatry.

Prideful Appearances

A simple place to begin would be the temptation to pridefully project the appearance of riches for the satisfaction of gaining the approval of others. Proverbs 13:7a states, "One pretends to be rich, yet has nothing." This proverb indicates that such a temptation has existed since the time of Solomon more than 3,000 years ago, yet it is likely more prevalent since the industrial and digital revolutions. In historically small villages of a hundred or fewer residents, it is reasonable to assume that the economic well-being of each individual was widely known in the community. When wealth was largely vested in flocks and fields (cf. Abraham in Gen 13:5–6; Job in Job 1:2–3; Joseph in Gen 47:20–23), then the economic status of neighbors could be externally observed. Even silver and gold as a display of wealth (Gen 13:2; 24:22; Jas 2:2) could only be seen by people close at hand or where news could travel by word-of-mouth. As a result, most everybody knew everyone in the village, and it was conceptually possible to be the wealthiest man in town.

In contrast, social media uniquely provides the temptation to display wealth through photographs that can be spread virally and essentially without any possibility of verification. For example, a man on social media driving an exotic sports car might not be rich if he must pay back an automobile loan essentially equal to the value of the car. Social media can give the appearance of wealth independent of the reality of the situation.

Trusting in Riches Rather than in God Alone

A second temptation especially addressed toward the rich would be to put trust in wealth rather than in God (1 Tim 6:17). On one hand, it is a positive development to have the means to store wealth for retirement in a Roth IRA account without significant risk of crops spoiling in storage, disease destroying herds of cattle, or of rust consuming buried coins. Jesus specifically warned against such risks to wealth on earth that could be lost to moths, rust, and thieves (Matt 6:19–21), and recent improvements in the rule of law and financial services have decreased these risks even more. FDIC insurance eliminates the risk of bank failure for many people. Mutual insurance on homes and automobiles lowers the costs of loss from accidents or fires just as healthcare insurance protects against catastrophic medical expenses. Life insurance reduces the risk of destitution faced by widows with small children in ways that were never possible before in history. Such financial products and technologies are not limited to an elite class anymore but are widely available to middle-class people.

Historically, people living on the edge of subsistence or at the whim of dangerous forces beyond their control tended to have a greater focus on the divine and cultivated a greater humility with a sense of dependence. Though many people in the United States still live paycheck to paycheck, riches present a greater temptation for misplaced trust than ever before in history.

Finding Satisfaction in Riches Rather than in God Alone

A third example would be finding satisfaction with riches. The Teacher of Ecclesiastes defines this condition with precision, saying that it is a gift from God when "God has given wealth and possessions and power to enjoy them" (Eccl 5:19). Instead, it is a vanity and grievous evil when "God gives wealth, possessions, and honor, so that he lacks nothing at all that he desires, *yet God has not given power to enjoy them*" (Eccl 6:1–2, emphasis added). The richest in the United States have unprecedented access to goods and services, yet because of relative comparisons to others, there is a lack of enjoyment or appreciation for wealth.

The likelihood of death by starvation in the United States has plummeted to near zero over the past two centuries because access to critical resources of even the poorest people has reached unprecedented heights. If people merely made absolute comparisons to true poverty, one would expect levels of satisfaction and gratitude to be the highest ever recorded. Instead, most people take for granted the baseline of wealth in their lives and focus instead on a relative comparison to the displayed riches of people around them. As a result, instead of record levels of gratitude, the United States is experiencing record levels of depression and dissatisfaction.

The Inherent Danger of Riches

The study of the rich could continue in looking at the effects of riches leading to separation or alienation from families (Gen 13:2–6), falling short of the levels of generosity that could be achieved (Ps 112:1–9; Prov 28:8; 1 Tim 6:9–18), the size of inheritance that could be left to one's heirs (cf. Prov 13:22), and so forth. For the sake of this limited study, however, an overarching concern should not be missed: Jesus was clear in his admonition that it is extremely difficult or even impossible for rich people to enter the kingdom of heaven (Matt 19:24; Mark 10:25; Luke 18:25). Further, Jesus declared that the cares of this world and deceitfulness of riches choke out spiritual seed and make it unfruitful (Matt 13:22). The truth of these passages should stand as a sober warning in the United States where even people living at the poverty level are wealthier than most people who have ever lived throughout history. The prophetic voice of the church must call out this growing peril.

Conclusions and Application for the Church in the Twenty-First Century

The Psalmist acknowledged the distinction between the groups of people who were rich and poor, but Augur in Proverbs 30:8 asks God to "give me neither poverty nor riches but give me only my daily bread." His goal was to avoid the unique temptations of the rich and of the poor, so he wrote, "Otherwise, I may have too much and disown you and say, 'Who is the LORD?' Or I may become poor and steal, and so dishonor the name of my God" (Prov 30:9). This recognizes the advantage of moderation for avoiding unique temptations of the rich and the poor, and still leaves much room for gratitude in recognizing that being in the middle class is much more conducive to human flourishing than ever before in history. Health care, dental care, quality housing, nutritious food, and so forth are above what was achieved by the richest people during the time of Augur (especially with material considerations such as air conditioning, anesthesia, access to travel, and advanced communication technologies).

In conclusion, pastors should prepare for sermons by exegeting the unchanging Word of God, but also remember to exegete the local congregation as it is ever-changing with culture. Indeed, the rate of cultural change has increased the past few decades, so this obligation is more important for the current generation of pastors than ever before.

The Academy can help the church with the next step in this intellectual work by scanning church sermons from the patristic era and the Reformation in order to better understand the temptations of those eras. Comparisons and contrasts from these sermons would be helpful in the preparation for sermons in local churches after the industrial revolution and in the coming social media age of the Metaverse.

5

Wealth, Poverty, and the Heavenly City in John's Apocalypse

Michael P. Naylor

Introduction

Promises of private jets, mansions, and exotic vehicles. Anticipation of luxury and affluence. Such are the alluring offers made by proponents of the prosperity gospel.[1] The Apocalypse of John, though not typically the central focus of such proponents, has been seen as providing support for their message of prosperity. The glittering "streets of gold" in particular seem to have captured the imagination. John Gray, in a 2018 interview defending pastors who enjoy an affluent lifestyle, stated, "We also understand that the reward in heaven is a mansion, streets paved with gold, gates that are made out of precious stones."[2] Kenneth Copeland Ministries describes the "wealth so immense that the streets are made of gold" and challenges the readers to discover that "the bridge has been built" so that "those boundless heavenly supplies could flow down to meet the needs in your life today" and "have all your needs met in abundance."[3]

---

[1] For a broad survey and response to the movement, see David W. Jones and Russell S. Woodbridge, *Health, Wealth, & Happiness: Has the Prosperity Gospel Overshadowed the Gospel of Christ?* (Kregel, 2011).

[2] Craig Hlavaty, "Lakewood Church's John Gray Defends the Wealth of High-Profile Pastors," *Houston Chronicle*, 24 January 2018, https://www.chron.com/lifestyle/houston-belief/article/Lakewood-Church-John-Gray-defends-pastor-wealth-12521278.php.

[3] Kenneth Copeland, "The Bridge between Two Worlds," Kenneth Copeland Ministries Europe, accessed 29 January 2022, https://kcm.org.uk/daily-devotional/the-bridge-between-two-worlds.

In his 2018 ethnographic study of the movement, Nathan Walton notes,

> Interviewees referenced biblical examples such as how Solomon's temple was adorned in the Hebrew Bible, the reference to heavenly streets of gold in the Book of Revelation, and Jesus' claim that there are many mansions in heaven. The logic is that if Christians are temples for the indwelling of the Holy Spirit, it is appropriate for them to embrace an aesthetic of wealth. Furthermore, if visible wealth is an eschatological reality that manifests as mansions and streets paved with gold, adherents believe it is appropriate to approximate that reality presently.[4]

Other studies of wealth and prosperity in Revelation, though not affirming the theological convictions of prosperity gospel proponents, have also concluded that John stresses the future wealth enjoyed by the people of God. M. Mathews argues that while at present John's readers face marginalization and poverty, they can anticipate the Deuteronomic (material) blessings that have been delayed until the arrival of this heavenly city.[5] J. N. Kraybill likewise asserts that "faithful believers now suffering poverty and powerlessness someday will enjoy wealth and safety in the New Jerusalem (21.9–27)."[6] C. Blomberg, in his otherwise helpful study of wealth and poverty, briefly concludes that this city reflects the "wealth of nations and all the luxuries that anyone could ever

---

4 Nathan Ivan Walton, "'Blessed and Highly Favored': The Theological Anthropology of the Prosperity Gospel" (PhD diss., University of Virginia, 2018), 105.

5 Mark D. Mathews, *Riches, Poverty, and the Faithful: Perspectives on Wealth in the Second Temple Period and the Apocalypse of John*, SNTSMS 154 (Cambridge University Press, 2013).

6 J. Nelson Kraybill, *Imperial Cults and Commerce in John's Apocalypse*, JSNTSup 132 (Sheffield, 1996), 25; and idem, *Apocalypse and Allegiance: Worship, Politics, and Devotion in the Book of Revelation* (Brazos, 2010), 177; see also Robert H. Gundry, "The New Jerusalem: People as Place, Not Place for People," *NovT* 29, no. 3 (1987): 261–262; Adela Yarbro Collins, *Crisis and Catharsis: The Power of the Apocalypse* (Westminster, 1984), 134; Greg Carey, "A Man's Choice: Wealth Imagery and the Two Cities of the Book of Revelation," in *A Feminist Companion to the Apocalypse of John,* ed. Amy-Jill Levine and Maria Mayo Robbins (T&T Clark, 2009), 147.

imagine."[7] R. Royalty, in his monograph, argues that Revelation reflects an ideology of wealth and seeks to entice readers with the surpassing wealth of the New Jerusalem.[8]

This essay will evaluate such claims, with a primary focus on the depiction of the New Jerusalem in Revelation 21:1–22:5. Attention will be given first, by way of overview, to descriptions of wealth and poverty in chapters 1–20. Next, we will consider the imagery of wealth in the depiction of the heavenly city. Finally, I will assess the claims of prosperity gospel advocates in the interpretation of this text in 21:1–22:5.[9]

Wealth and Poverty in Revelation 1–20: An Overview

Space does not permit a full exploration of references to wealth and poverty in Revelation 1–20, but a few comments are necessary to frame the discussion concerning the New Jerusalem.

First, concerns with wealth and poverty can be observed in the messages to the seven churches. Although arguably not the central issue in chapters two and three, the concern with wealth surfaces most explicitly in the messages to Smyrna (2:8–11) and Laodicea (3:14–22).[10] In the message to Smyrna, the congregation is facing poverty (πτωχεία), along with tribulation and slander.[11] The

---

7 Craig L. Blomberg, *Neither Poverty nor Riches: A Biblical Theology of Possessions*, NSBT 7 (InterVarsity, 1999), 238.

8 Robert M. Royalty Jr., *The Streets of Heaven: The Ideology of Wealth in the Apocalypse of John* (Mercer University Press, 1998).

9 Although the focus in this essay is upon descriptions of wealth, Revelation likewise does not promise a lack of suffering for the believer. Rather, believers face the very real threat of suffering and persecution (see, e.g., 1:9; 2:9–10; 6:9–11; 7:13–14; 13:9–10; 17:6; 20:4).

10 The false teaching associated with "Balaam" (2:14), the "Nicolaitans" (2:6, 15), and "Jezebel" (2:20–25) may have promised economic benefits through spiritual compromise.

11 R. Mounce, following R. Trench, suggests that the πτωχεία should be understood in a more absolute sense, in distinction from the term πένης, which could suggest more relative levels of poverty. Robert H. Mounce, *The Book of Revelation*, rev. ed., NICNT (Eerdmans, 1998), 74; Richard C. Trench, *Synonyms of the New Testament*, 9th ed. (Eerdmans, 1953), 129. The term, however, does not appear to carry this distinction in the NT. So Grant R. Osborne, *Revelation*, BECNT (Baker, 2002), 129.

assessment of Christ concerning the reality of their situation provides a helpful perspective—despite their apparent poverty, they are truly rich.[12] The possession of wealth is not condemned here, but neither is the accumulation of future wealth promised.[13] Instead, the people are comforted concerning the struggle with material poverty by the recognition of their true spiritual riches. This correlation is not always the reality,[14] but for the congregation in Smyrna, such was the case.

The message to Laodicea presents a different picture, as the congregation is rebuked for their self-sufficiency. The attitude of the congregation is captured in the imputed speech in 3:17,[15] and there may be an allusion to the reputation of the city as wealthy.[16] Unlike Smyrna, the attitude and perhaps the experience of the congregation reflected the wider culture of the city. Christ invites them to acquire from him gold, garments, and salve, and these items are best understood as representative of spiritual wealth rather than material commodities to be acquired.[17]

The next major text to consider is the depiction of Babylon the Great in Revelation 17–18. This city is depicted in 17:4 (cf.

---

[12] M. Mathews identifies the reversal present in the language found in the messages to Smyrna and Laodicea. M. Mathews, "The Epistle of Enoch and Revelation 2:1–3:22," in *Reading Revelation in Context: John's Apocalypse and Second Temple Judaism*, ed. Ben C. Blackwell, John K. Goodrich, and Jason Maston (Zondervan, 2019), 49. However, his assertion that this refers to future material wealth fails to capture the assertion in both passages. Rather than future material prosperity, 2:9 and 3:17–18 recognize the present possession (2:9) or offer (3:17–18) of spiritual wealth.

[13] So David A. deSilva, *Seeing Things John's Way: The Rhetoric of the Book of Revelation* (Westminster John Knox, 2009), 59.

[14] Other Second Temple Jewish texts use the language of poverty to describe the righteous (see Pss. Sol. 5.2, 11; 10.6; 15.1; 1QpHab XII; see also *NIDNTTE*, 4.183). John does not associate poverty exclusively with the righteous, however, as both rich and poor participate in worshipping the image of the beast (Rev 13:16).

[15] As G. K. Beale notes, they may have viewed their spiritual condition as being satisfactory due to their material wealth. G. K. Beale, *The Book of Revelation*, NIGTC (Eerdmans, 1999), 304.

[16] See Osborne, *Revelation*, 201, 208–210.

[17] Cf. Isa 55:1. So Ian Paul, *Revelation*, TNTC 20 (InterVarsity, 2018), 115; Buist M. Fanning, *Revelation*, ZECNT (Zondervan, 2020), 188; Osborne, *Revelation*, 210.

18:16) as a woman of great wealth, dressed in purple and scarlet,[18] adorned with gold, jewels, and pearls,[19] and holding a golden cup.[20] John depicts Babylon as a woman of great wealth and prosperity, enticing the kings and earth-dwellers alike (17:2; 18:3).[21] Revelation 18:3 makes clear the association of her immorality and riches,[22] and the items mentioned in 18:11–17 provide insight into the wealth of the great city. Although it depends somewhat on the trade described in Ezekiel 27:12–14, this list also reflects trade in the first-century world.[23] Some of the items listed, such as marble, cinnamon, spice, myrrh, and frankincense, suggest an origination at the outer limits of the empire.[24] Particularly jarring is the inclusion of "slaves" at the end of the list alongside cattle, sheep, horses, and chariots.[25] This structure indicates the devaluing of human life and the real nature of the relationship between Rome and the peoples of the empire.[26] For the people of God, the appropriate

---

18 These colors help to highlight the wealth (and, possibly, the royalty) of this woman. See Osborne, *Revelation*, 611; Fanning, *Revelation*, 438; Paul, *Revelation*, 281.

19 There is not a clear source for this imagery in the OT. B. Rossing posits that the imagery is drawn from stock imagery of the "unfaithful woman." See B. Rossing, *The Choice between Two Cities: Whore, Bride, and Empire in the Apocalypse*, HTS 48 (Trinity, 1999), 77–78.

20 The exterior (golden) contrasts memorably with the contents: it is full of abominations and the impurities of her sexual immorality. So Paul, *Revelation*, 282.

21 The depiction in Rev 17 may also reflect imagery drawn from depictions of the goddess Roma. See David E. Aune, *Revelation 17–22*, WBC 52C (Thomas Nelson, 1998), 920–928.

22 On the relationship between economics and idolatry, see Beale, *Revelation*, 856–857, 912; Kraybill, *Imperial Cults and Commerce*.

23 I. Provan links the passage in Rev 18 exclusively with Ezek 27. See I. Provan, "Foul Spirits, Fornication and Finance: Revelation 18 from an Old Testament Perspective," *JSNT* 64 (1996): 81–100. However, sufficient detail may be seen that indicates that John was engaging Roman imperial power as well. See Richard Bauckham, *The Climax of Prophecy: Studies on the Book of Revelation* (T&T Clark, 1993), 338–383; Allen D. Callahan, "Apocalypse as Critique of Political Economy: Some Notes on Revelation 18," *HBT* 21 (1999): 46–65.

24 Osborne, *Revelation*, 648–649.

25 See Craig R. Koester, "Roman Slave Trade and the Critique of Babylon in Revelation 18," *CBQ* 70, no. 4 (2008): 766–786; Osborne, *Revelation*, 650.

26 See Douglas E. Oakman, "The Ancient Economy and St. John's

response is neither to marvel over her wealth (cf. 17:6b-7) nor participate in her sins (18:4-8).[27] The rebuke is not directed simply against the accumulation of wealth in and of itself, but for the wicked city, the promise of wealth and luxury is one way in which she entices the people of the world.[28]

Finally, depictions of God, Christ, and the heavenly throne room use images of jewels and precious metals. The depiction of Jesus in Revelation 1:12-20 features a long robe and a golden sash. Likewise, Revelation 4 is notable for the imagery of precious jewels. The appearance of the one seated on the throne is described as like "jasper" and "carnelian," and the throne is surrounded by a rainbow that appears like an emerald (4:3), with a crystal sea of glass before the throne (4:6). The twenty-four elders, who encircle the throne and worship God, wear golden crowns, and Jesus is ascribed "wealth" in the acclamation in 5:12.[29] Other heavenly beings are associated with golden objects, such as bowls of incense (5:8), a censer (8:3), an altar (8:3), sashes (15:6), and bowls (15:7). Royalty argues that these features depict Jesus/God in Hellenistic/Roman terms highlighting the wealth of a monarch.[30] Although these features could have conveyed status and wealth, it is more likely that John has utilized these elements due to their appearance in texts such as Daniel 7, Daniel 10, and Ezekiel 1.[31] Likewise, the various golden objects in the heavenly sanctuary allude to the use

---

Apocalypse," *List* 28 (1993): 200-214; deSilva, *Seeing Things John's Way*, 45-46.

27 Royalty's charge that John demonstrates no concern for social justice (*Streets*, 71, 183) does not give sufficient attention to this command to "come out" from Babylon the Great. See Royalty, *The Streets of Heaven*, 71, 183. By "coming out" from this city, Christ-followers are refusing to participate in the immoral and idolatrous actions of this wicked city, including the unjust ways the city exploits the peoples of the earth. The command reflects similar calls in Gen 19:12-22 and Jer 50:8-10; 51:6-10, 45-48; cf. Isa 48:20-22; 52:11-12. See Fanning, *Revelation*, 459; deSilva, *Seeing Things John's Way*, 72-75.

28 See Callahan, "Apocalypse as Critique," 57, 64.

29 Although this could include material wealth, spiritual wealth is likely primary based on the statements in Rev 2:9 and 3:18.

30 Royalty, *The Streets of Heaven*, 97-101, 178-181.

31 So Mathews, *Riches, Poverty, and the Faithful*, 170; see Michael P. Naylor, *Complexity and Creativity: John's Presentation of Jesus in the Book of Revelation*, Gorgias Biblical Studies 69 (Gorgias, 2018), 142-145.

of the golden instruments in the tabernacle/temple.[32]

The preceding survey has yielded several points. First, John points to true spiritual wealth, as can be seen in the messages to Smyrna and Laodicea. Second, John sharply rebukes "Babylon" for her exploitive accumulation of wealth (along with her other sins). By way of application, the response of the people of God is to "come out" from Babylon and refuse to associate with her sins. Finally, alleged images of "wealth" in the descriptions of God and/or Jesus serve to identify John's vision with antecedent texts and advance the depiction of the heavenly throne room as a sanctuary.

New Jerusalem

In light of these preceding images and passages, we now turn to the primary text of focus: John's description of the New Jerusalem in Revelation 21:1–22:5.

Images of Wealth in the New Jerusalem

As John begins his description in 21:9, he is taken to a "high mountain," where he sees the city descending from heaven.[33] The city is described as "having the glory of God," a theme that will prove to be significant in the account that follows. It is here that the first image of wealth appears; namely, her radiance is as a precious stone, like a crystal stone of "jasper."

The initial description of the walls and gates in 21:12–18 features several notable details concerning the size of the city and the walls. The walls, unnecessary given the absence of evil in the new creation (21:8), are likely intended to convey the security of this eternal city.[34] The walls are described as being built of

---

32 See Sung-Min Park, "More than a Regained Eden: The New Jerusalem as the Ultimate Portrayal of Eschatological Blessedness and Its Implication for the Understanding of the Book of Revelation" (PhD diss., Trinity Evangelical Divinity School, 1995), 213.

33 A number of features indicate that the New Jerusalem provides an intended contrast with "Babylon."

34 So Osborne, *Revelation*, 749–750; Pilchan Lee, *The New Jerusalem in the Book of Revelation: A Study of Revelation 21–22 in the Light of Its Background in*

"jasper," reinforcing the prior description of the city in verse 11. Further, the city is described as being constructed of "pure gold" (χρυσίον καθαρόν) like "pure glass" (ὑάλῳ καθαρῷ), an unusual feature, given that gold is not typically transparent.[35] As John advances to the foundations of the city in verses 19–21, he begins with the general description of "every kind of jewel" and then enumerates the twelve different types on each respective layer of the foundation.[36]

Revelation 21:21 focuses on the gates and streets. Introduced in verses 12–13 as being inscribed with the names of the sons of Israel and distributed equally on the four sides of the city, the twelve gates are now identified as twelve individual pearls. The streets or perhaps better the main plaza or "great street"[37] is likewise impressive. John again uses the language of "pure gold" (cf. 21:18), described as being "transparent, like glass" (ὑάλῳ διαυγής), recalling the "clear glass" (ὑάλῳ καθαρῷ) in 21:18.

An additional image in 21:24 contributes to the splendor of the city as the nations "walk by the light of the city" and the kings "bring their glory into it." Within the narrative, this provides a striking contrast with previous depictions of the nations in active opposition to God and his people.[38] This image in 21:24 is likely drawn from Isaiah 60, which anticipates God's restoration of his people. Isaiah 60 describes the camels (60:6), gold (60:6, 9, 17), frankincense (60:6), flocks (60:7), silver (60:9, 17), various

---

Jewish Tradition, WUNT 2.129 (Mohr Siebeck, 2001), 276–281.

35 The collocation of "gold" and "streets" in the discussion of Jerusalem in Tob 13:16 could be the source of this imagery, although this is not conclusive. Alternative explanations will be considered in turn.

36 Uncertainty about the exact identifications of the stones can be seen in the variation among English translations, particularly concerning the third, fifth, sixth, and tenth stones. See Robert G. Bratcher and Howard A. Hatton, *A Handbook on the Revelation to John*, UBS Handbook Series (United Bible Societies, 1993), 308; Una Jart, "The Precious Stones in the Revelation of St. John xxi.18–21," *ST* 24 (1970): 150–181. The source of this imagery will be considered in turn.

37 The term in Greek (πλατεῖα) is singular. Although this could be a collective singular, it likely refers to the main plaza, public square (so Fanning, *Revelation*, 543), or main street (so Osborne, *Revelation*, 759) running through the center of the city.

38 See, for example, Rev 6:15; 13:7; 16:14; 17:15; 20:8.

varieties of wood (60:13), bronze (60:17), and iron (60:17) brought to the city. Of particular interest is the statement in Isaiah 60:11, where the people bring "the wealth of the nations" and the "kings [are] led in procession" to the city. Other Jewish texts develop this theme. Tobit 13:11 describes the flow of gifts from inhabitants of the remotest parts of the earth to Jerusalem. 4Q504 IV depicts the nations bringing silver, gold, gems, and every precious thing, and 1QM XII, 11–18 likewise reflects the subjugation of nations before Israel and the presence of gold and precious stones in the palaces of Zion.

As can be seen with this brief survey, a variety of precious and costly materials are used in Revelation 21:1–22:5 in the description of the New Jerusalem. The city, in both its size and construction, is indeed impressive.

Wealth and the Heavenly City: An Assessment

The presence of the imagery of wealth in the heavenly city may appear to support the thesis that John simply describes the delay of material satisfaction to the eternal state or is identifying the true material wealth available to believers, as suggested by proponents of the prosperity gospel. Such a reading, perhaps distracted by the glittering of the jewels, may miss John's point in his portrayal of the New Jerusalem. In fact, close attention to the depiction of the heavenly city and the sources of the imagery confirms that the cultic nature of the city, rather than the material wealth, should be seen as the primary point of focus within this text.

The Sanctuary

First, several features indicate that John is concerned with the function of the city as a sanctuary. As John describes his vision of the heavenly city descending as a bride adorned for her husband, he hears the proclamation from heaven that now the "dwelling place of God is with man" and that "God will dwell with them, and they will be his people, and God himself will be with them as their God" (21:3). The occurrences of σκηνή and the related verb σκηνόω in verse 3 likely allude to the Tabernacle as the physical expression of the dwelling of God with his people in the Mosaic covenant. The rest of the announcement is drawn from Leviticus 26:12 and identifies the New Jerusalem as the climactic expression of the theme of God dwelling with his people.[39]

Given this reference to the "dwelling" of God in Revelation 21:3, one might expect to find a description of a "temple" building, especially in light of the attention given to the temple in Ezekiel's vision.[40] John, however, makes explicit the *lack* of temple (21:22). Rather, God and the Lamb[41] *are* the temple, and this identification indicates that the role of the temple in mediating the presence of God among his people is no longer necessary.[42]

Further to this, the geometric shape of the city described in 21:15–17 alludes to the nature of the entire city as a sanctuary. John describes the city as laying in a square, with the height of the city equal to the measurements of the sides. This cubic shape mirrors the shape of the inner sanctuary in the tabernacle/temple.[43] These aspects indicate that the city as a whole functions as an eternal sanctuary.[44]

Priests and the Worship of God

Beyond the presence of language and imagery that identifies the

---

39 See also 11Q19–20, 29.

40 See Ezek 40–48; see G. K. Beale, *The Temple and the Church's Mission: A Biblical Theology of the Dwelling Place of God*, NSBT 17 (InterVarsity, 2004), 351.

41 See Naylor, *Complexity and Creativity*, 232–237, 247–256.

42 A similar conflation of city and temple can be seen in 4 Ezra. See Jonathan Moo, "4 Ezra and Revelation 21:1–22:5: Paradise City," in *Reading Revelation in Context: John's Apocalypse and Second Temple Judaism*, ed. Ben C. Blackwell, John K. Goodrich, and Jason Maston (Zondervan, 2019), 171.

43 This appears to be a development of the "foursquare" imagery in Ezek 41–48 (see, esp., 45:2 and 48:20). See Osborne, *Revelation*, 752–753; G. R. Beasley-Murray, *The Book of Revelation* (1981; repr., Wipf & Stock, 2010), 322; Mathias Rissi, *The Future of the World: An Exegetical Study of Revelation 19.11–22.15*, SBT 23 (Allenson, 1966), 62; Dave Mathewson, *A New Heaven and a New Earth: The Meaning and Function of the Old Testament in Revelation 21.1–22.5*, JSNTSup 238 (Sheffield, 2003), 107; Brian J. Tabb, *All Things New: Revelation as Canonical Capstone*, NSBT 48 (InterVarsity, 2019), 178.

44 So Osborne, *Revelation*, 760.

city as a sanctuary, several details in 21:1–22:5 identify the role of the inhabitants as priests. First, the inhabitants of the city are described as those who "serve" him in 22:3–4. The term used, λατρεύω, carries cultic overtones of religious service, or worship, rendered to God.[45] John uses the term earlier in Revelation 7:15 to refer to the great multitude who serve before the throne of God. This text builds upon the earlier imagery in Revelation 4–5 of the scene of heavenly worship before the throne in heaven. The term also appears in Judges and Daniel in the LXX with the meaning of offering religious devotion to various deities.[46] Within the NT, religious connotations can likewise be seen.[47] The use in Revelation 22:3–4, then, suggests that the "service" offered by the inhabitants is worship.

Other expressions in Revelation likewise anticipate a priestly role for the people of God. In the doxology in Revelation 1:6, Jesus is hailed as the one who "made us to be a kingdom, priests to his God and father." This is later repeated in the "new song" of Revelation 5:9–10 and in the pronouncement in Revelation 20:6. The language is drawn from Exodus 19:6, albeit with some modification. The promise to the overcomer in Revelation 3:12 to be established as a pillar in the "temple of my God" should be seen in the same manner as anticipating the eternal abiding of the believer in the New Jerusalem.

Next, the precious stones in Revelation 21 may also reflect priestly imagery. The text of Isaiah 54:11–12 clearly appears to be in view in the general depiction of the city,[48] but the enumeration of the twelve stones is significant. Although some suggest that the signs of the zodiac are the source of the list,[49] a connection with

---

45 BDAG, 587; Mathewson, *New Heaven and New Earth*, 205.
46 See, in the LXX, Judg 2:11, 13, 19; 3:6, 7; Dan 3:12, 14, 17, 18, 95; 6:17, 21.
47 See, e.g., Luke 2:37; 4:8; Rom 1:25; Heb 8:5; 9:9, 14.
48 In this text, the stones of the city are set in turquoise, the foundations with sapphire, the pinnacles of agate, the gates with carbuncles, and the walls with precious stones.
49 On the former, see R. H. Charles, *A Critical and Exegetical Commentary on the Revelation of John*, ICC (T&T Clark, 1920), 2:167–168; Austin Farrer, *A Rebirth of Images: The Making of St. John's Apocalypse* (1963; repr., Wipf & Stock, 2006), 216–236; Jeffrey Marshall Vogelgesang, "The Interpretation of Ezekiel in

the ephod of the high priest in Exodus 28:17–21 (cf. 39:10–14) is more likely. The setting of twelve stones in gold and the commonalities in the lists suggest a stronger (and primary) connection with Exodus, and the description of the king of Tyre in Ezekiel 28:13, likely in view as well, seems to draw from these texts in Exodus.[50] If these texts have indeed influenced the depiction in Revelation 21, the identification of the stones with the city itself would indicate that all the inhabitants now serve in this significant role as priests.[51]

Finally, the description of the nations and kings in Revelation 21 reflects a concern with worship in the New Jerusalem. Although "glory" and "honor" could be understood as a reference to great wealth, the use of the term "glory" elsewhere in Revelation suggests that worship is instead in view.[52] In chapter 11, the inhabitants of the "great city" gave "glory" to God after his vindication of the two witnesses. Likewise, the proclamation of the "eternal gospel" in Revelation 14:7 consists of the call to "fear God and give him glory" (cf. 15:4; 19:7). Finally, a lack of repentance is

---

the Book of Revelation" (PhD thesis, Harvard University, 1985), 99–100. On the latter, see Beale, *Revelation*, 1087–1088; Rissi, *Future of the World*, 72; Aune, *Revelation 17–22*, 1165, 1187.

50 See Beale, *Revelation*, 1080–1090; Osborne, *Revelation*, 755–756; Tabb, *All Things New*, 178–179. The lack of a precise match in the list of stones is not necessarily problematic, as these could vary during the second temple period; see Josephus, *Ant.* 3.7.5; idem, *J.W.* 5.5.7; Mathewson, *New Heaven and New Earth*, 131. Evidence for a connection with the zodiac is not strong; see William W. Reader, "The Twelve Jewels of Revelation 21:19–20: Tradition History and Modern Interpretations," *JBL* 100, no. 3 (1981): 455; cf. also J. A. Draper, "The Twelve Apostles as Foundation Stones of the Heavenly Jerusalem and the Foundation of the Qumran Community," *Neot* 22, no. 1 (1988): 44; contra Charles, *Revelation of John*, 2:167–168; Beasley-Murray, *Revelation*, 325. The presence of gold throughout the city may also allude to the description of the temple in 1 Kgs 6:20ff. (see Beale, *Temple*, 370; Beasley-Murray, *Revelation*, 324) and the use of gold in articles found in the tabernacle (so Park, "More than a Regained Eden," 214).

51 4QpIsa[d] makes a similar connection between the stones and the community. See Celia Deutsch, "Transformation of Symbols: The New Jerusalem in Rv 21:1–22:5," *ZNW* 78 (1987): 113–115; Draper, "Twelve Apostles," 52–56; Lee, *New Jerusalem*, 285–286.

52 See Osborne, *Revelation*, 763; Beale, *Revelation*, 1096; contra Fanning (*Revelation*, 545) and Kraybill (*Imperial Cults and Commerce*, 222), who see this as the things produced by the nations.

described as failing to give God glory (16:9). In light of these expressions, it is best to conclude that John is describing not the flow of material wealth but rather the worship offered to God and the Lamb. This suggests a spiritual, rather than material, interpretation of Isaiah 60, perhaps with a focus on 60:6b.[53] Within Revelation, then, two very different outcomes for the nations/kings are depicted: destruction for those in allegiance with Satan and his forces[54] or redemption through conversion.[55] Of central concern in this passage is not the material wealth of the city but rather than the spiritual fate of the nations and kings.[56]

These various elements affirm the priestly nature of the people of God. Along with the aforementioned "sanctuary" imagery, the priestly imagery helps to affirm that the spiritual significance of the city stands as primary in the description of the New Jerusalem. The significance of the precious materials may now be revisited.

---

53 See Allan J. McNicol, *Conversion of the Nations in Revelation*, LNTS 438 (T&T Clark, 2011), 79; see also Jan Fekkes, *Isaiah and Prophetic Traditions in the Book of Revelation: Visionary Antecedents and Their Development*, JSNTSup 93 (Sheffield Academic, 1994), 270; Beale, *Revelation*, 1095.

54 See Rev 6:15; 10:11; 11:2, 9, 18; 13:7; 14; 16:12, 14, 19; 17:2, 12, 15, 18; 18:3, 9, 23; 19:15, 18, 19; 20:8. The defeat of the nations is frequently articulated through the lens of Ps 2; see Rev 2:27; 11:18; 12:5; 19:15, 19. So McNicol, *Conversion of the Nations*, 41–56.

55 See Rev 5:9; 7:9; 15:3–4; 22:2.

56 The precise means by which this is accomplished is debated. Some posit that John is depicting universal salvation, where the formerly hostile nations and kings repent and migrate from the place of judgment to the eternal city; see Rissi, *Future of the World*, 78–79, 83; Vogelgesang, "Interpretation of Ezekiel," 103–105. Bauckham, in his significant study of this theme, stresses a widespread conversion of the nations through the suffering witness of the church; see Bauckham, *Climax of Prophecy*, 238–337. Beale, Schnabel, and Gundry resolve the tension by stressing that it is the redeemed from the nations (see 5:9) that then become the "nations" and "kings" depicted in 21:24. See Beale, *Revelation*, 1097; Eckhard J. Schnabel, "John and the Future of the Nations," *BBR* 12, no. 2 (2002): 243–271; Gundry, "New Jerusalem"; see also McNicol, *Conversion of the Nations*. Morales and Mathewson stress the rhetorical function in calling the nations to repentance. See Jon Morales, *Christ, Shepherd of the Nations: The Nations as Narrative Character and Audience in John's Apocalypse*, LNTS 577 (T&T Clark, 2018); Dave Mathewson, "The Destiny of the Nations in Revelation 21:1–22:5: A Reconsideration," *TynBul* 53, no. 1 (2002): 121–142.

Gold, Jewels, and the Glory of God

Although the use of costly materials in the description is striking, careful attention must be paid to the function of the imagery in the text. The first jewel mentioned, "jasper," appears in a simile used to describe the splendor of the glory of God (Rev 21:11). John uses a similar expression to describe the radiance and beauty of God in his throne room (see 4:3).[57] The emphasis on jasper, highlighted in 21:11, helps to link the glory of God (4:3) with the city (21:18, 19).[58] Additionally, the presence of God's glory, as identified in 21:11 and 21:23, frames the description of the city. Although John draws from texts depicting the radiance of the city (Isa 60:19–20; Tob 13:11), he deploys this imagery to describe the glory of God's presence rather than the wealth of the city.

The glory of the Lord is often described as a brightness of light or a cloud that overwhelms the space in which it is manifested.[59] Prior sanctuaries, such as the tabernacle, Solomon's temple, and Zerubbabel's temple, were constructed with a series of curtains and/or walls that served to separate the people from the manifestation of God's glory.[60] The presence of the glory of God in the New Jerusalem expresses the fulfillment of Isaiah 60:19[61] and may also allude to the vision of Zechariah where the city will be inhabited by a great multitude and will be protected by the Lord, who declares that he will be the "glory in her midst" (Zech 2:5). In this heavenly city, the glory of God enlightens the entire city. The function of the costly materials should then be revisited. Rather than stressing a promise of material wealth, the gold and precious stones serve the purpose of both describing the magnificence of God's glory

---

57 This feature is not unique to Revelation (see, e.g., Ezek 1:4, 22, 26–28).

58 So Osborne, *Revelation*, 749; Beasley-Murray, *Revelation*, 319. Jasper, typically opaque, is described as "shining like crystal," perhaps signifying a diamond. As Beale notes, however, the focus is on the luminosity; See Beale, *Revelation*, 1067–1068.

59 See, e.g., Exod 24:15–16; 40:34–35; 1 Kgs 8:10–12; Isa 6:1–4; Ezek 43:2–5; Isa 60:1–2; cf. also 1 En. 14:20–21; 2 En. 65:8–10; Ps.-Philo 26:13.

60 So Craig R. Koester, "Revelation's Vision of New Jerusalem: God's Life-Giving Reign for the World," *WW* 40, no. 2 (2020): 115.

61 So Rissi, *Future of the World*, 61.

(Rev 21:11) and facilitating the permeation of this glory through all parts of the city.[62] Several of the precious stones, such as "jasper" (along with the descriptive "like crystal" in 21:11), "sapphire," "emerald," "topaz," and "amethyst," are translucent and would allow light to pass through the walls of the city.[63] The curious description of the gold as clear (21:18, 21) may also be explained by this aim within the passage. This gold is not only noteworthy for its purity; it also allows the glory of God to shine through the material throughout the sanctuary-city.[64] These precious stones and transparent gold help to facilitate the spread of this radiant glory throughout the entirety of the city, to the extent that no physical light source is needed (21:23; cf. 22:5).[65]

Conclusions

John challenges his readers to carefully consider their participation in the systems of the world, including those who offer material wealth as enticement. In light of the cultic language both framing and permeating Revelation 21:1–22:5, concerns with the spiritual nature of this city appear to be primary. Imagery of wealth, clearly present in antecedent texts such as Isaiah 54:11–12, Isaiah 60, and Tobit 13:11–16, has been deployed in Revelation 21:1–22:5 to communicate the presence of the glory of God rather than the material prosperity of the city or its inhabitants. As Mathewson rightly notes, "Although it is apparent that the new Jerusalem is to be understood as the compensation for the disadvantaged readers

---

62 See Park, "More than a Regained Eden," 211–213. And, in contrast to the merchants who lament the lost transactional wealth they had gained from Babylon (cf. Rev 18:11–17a), the city possesses inherent value.

63 See BDAG, 52, 465, 913, 933, 1010. Carey notes the prevalence of materials that "shine" or "reflect light" rather than absorb light; see Carey, "A Man's Choice," 156–157; see also Ibson T. Beckwith, *The Apocalypse of John* (Baker, 1967), 762; Fekkes, *Isaiah and Prophetic Traditions*, 251. The preference for these types of materials supports the assertion that the function of these materials, rather than wealth, is primary in John's view.

64 So Osborne, *Revelation*, 755.

65 So Rissi, *Future of the World*, 62; Beale, *Revalation*, 1079. Ps.-Philo 25–26 stresses the role that the stones, associated with the twelve tribes, play in providing light to the righteous.

in Asia Minor, it does not logically follow that their reward must be in terms of material or monetary remuneration."[66] Readings of this text that see wealth as a primary motivating factor for the Christ-follower, whether at present, as in the case of the prosperity gospel, or in the future, have missed the greater theological point that John is making concerning the climax of the theme of God dwelling with his people. The significance of this city lies not in the presence of great wealth and material *prosperity* but rather in the unhindered and unmediated *presence* of the glory of God now dwelling with his people.

---

66 Mathewson, *New Heaven and New Earth*, 141.

6

How Shall We Sing the Prosperity Gospel's Song in an Evangelical Church?

Matthew D. Westerholm

WHILE THERE ARE several worthy avenues to explore at the intersection between this book's topic and my academic field of study (corporate worship), this chapter investigates the controversial relationship between evangelical churches and the songs associated with what is often called the prosperity gospel.[1] We pursue the investigation with three questions:

1. Why do evangelical churches sing prosperity gospel songs?
2. Why do critics think evangelical churches should absolutely never sing songs from this movement?
3. How should we think about this?

Why Do Evangelical Churches Sing the Songs from the Prosperity Gospel Movement?

Upon initial reflection, interactions between these two movements seem very unlikely. What could the loose network of Pentecostal broadcasters and megachurches of the prosperity gospel have in common with the local churches who identify with the theological and intellectual tradition of evangelicalism? They attend neither the same conferences nor educational institutions. Perhaps it is surprising, then, that despite the vanishingly small institutional

---

1 This chapter is based on a presentation at the Evangelical Theological Society annual meeting on the topic of "wealth and poverty," held (to the delight of biblical typologists) in Ft. Worth, in November of 2021.

overlap, Church Copyright Licensing International (CCLI) data shows that many evangelical churches sing songs that originated within organizations affiliated with the prosperity gospel.

Why do evangelical churches sing songs from the prosperity gospel movement? In brief, because the prosperity gospel movement and evangelical churches actually share many cultural values. How this seemingly unlikely claim could possibly be true we address by tracing, first, the popularity, then the history of the prosperity gospel movement, before consolidating our findings with a four-part definition.

Popularity

As we discuss the shared values between evangelicalism and the prosperity gospel movement, it is important to note the great popularity of the prosperity gospel. A 2006 poll in *Time* magazine reported that 17 percent of adult U.S. Christians identified themselves as part of the prosperity gospel movement.[2] Beyond that sort of self-identification, 31 percent of Christians agreed with the statement "God increases the riches of those who give." An even higher percentage, two-thirds of Christians surveyed, agreed that "God wants people to prosper." In a different 2008 survey, the Pew Charitable Trust reported that 43 percent of Christians surveyed agreed with the statement, "the faithful receive health and wealth." The same survey found that 75 percent of Latino believers across all Christian denominations agreed with the statement, "God will grant financial success and good health to all believers who have enough faith."[3]

Hopefully, this addresses one of the common criticisms of

---

2 David Van Biema and Jeff Chu, "Does God Want You to Be Rich?," *Time* 168, no. 12 (September 2006): 48–56, http://content.time.com/time/magazine/article/0,9171,1533448,00.html, cited in Kate Bowler, *Blessed: A History of the American Prosperity Gospel* (Oxford University Press, 2013), 6.

3 Pew Hispanic Center and Pew Forum on Religion and Public Life, "Changing Faiths: Latinos and the Transformation of American Religion," Pew Research Center, 25 April 2007, https://www.pewforum.org/2007/04/25/changing-faiths-latinos-and-the-transformation-of-american-religion-2, cited in Bowler, *Blessed*, 6.

prosperity gospel songs—that these songs are a sinister attempt to try to pull people (especially young people) out of evangelical churches and relocate them into the prosperity gospel movement. These surveys indicate a different narrative: churches hold many people who already believe core tenets of the prosperity gospel. The songs cannot be blamed for convincing otherwise wary people against their better judgment because these contemporary songs are too recent to explain the pervasive and popular nature of these doctrines in North American Christianity, including American evangelicalism. Older answers are needed. How did it get this way?

The History of the Prosperity Gospel

The prosperity gospel formed with the intermingling of two different strands of American religious thought: the New Thought of the early nineteenth century and the Pentecostalism of the early twentieth century.[4] While Pentecostalism has been studied in great depth and is more familiar, fewer people are familiar with New Thought, even though it may be a more pervasive and influential religious movement.[5]

Mystic beliefs have been held across cultures, geographies, and eras of history, including beliefs that a person could arrange certain objects in the physical universe in a superstitious way in order to produce a good relationship with the spiritual forces in the world. This includes all manner of tokens or talismans—four-leaf clovers, rabbits' feet, lucky pennies or coins, upturned horseshoes—as charms to receive good luck or divine favor.

---

4 Kate Bowler and Wen Reagan, "Bigger, Better, Louder: The Prosperity Gospel's Impact on Contemporary Worship," *Religion and American Culture: A Journal of Interpretation* 24, no. 2 (Summer 2014): 187–188.

5 Discussions of Pentecostalism include R. G. Robins, *Pentecostalism in America* (Praeger, 2010); Grant Wacker, *Heaven Below: Early Pentecostals and American Culture* (Harvard University Press, 2003). For discussion of music, worship, and Pentecostalism, see Monique Ingalls and Amos Young, eds., *The Spirit of Praise: Music and Worship in Global Pentecostal-Charismatic Christianity* (The Pennsylvania State University Press, 2015); Randall J. Stephens, *The Devil's Music: How Christians Inspired, Condemned, and Embraced Rock 'n' Roll* (Harvard University Press, 2018).

Historian Catherine Albanese has traced the evolution that occurred after the Civil War from what she calls "material magic" to what she calls "mental magic."[6] This movement was called "New Thought" or sometimes "Mind-Power."[7] Moving away from traditional mystical beliefs that physical things controlled the physical realm, the new folk religion increasingly highlighted the mental, believing that right thoughts and right words create or manifest realities. Soon, this folk religion developed a Christianized version. While many Christians have prayed with a desire to encounter divine persons and power, some Christians have desired a more direct production of their desired results. Using a form of this New Thought, many self-identified Christians worked to command the physical and spiritual planes of reality through the interior world of thought, imagination, meditation, and prayer.[8]

The 1930s saw New Thought distinctives combine with the Pentecostal movement. Earlier Pentecostals approached New Thought with skepticism, as it was not explicitly Christian. Elements of this mental magic approach, however, grew increasingly popular during this time, and it is not difficult to see why. As the nation recovered from the Great Depression, many Americans were looking to explain why some people had fallen into great financial ruin while other people had succeeded. Many stories during that time evoked imagery of people "pulling themselves up by their bootstraps" through hard work and self-belief, and New Thought principles became widespread throughout the culture. As one example, the Disney corporation began to make feature films, such as 1940's *Pinocchio*, capturing the American imagination with stories of people who believe in themselves and listen to their internal guide rather than the outside world. These narratives often suggested and sometimes explicitly claimed that their successful reality was caused by believing in their own dreams. People succeeded as they believed in themselves, spoke positive words of belief, and

---

6 Catherine L. Albanese, *A Republic of Mind and Spirit: A Cultural History of American Metaphysical Religion* (Yale University Press, 2007), 7–16.

7 Bowler's term, taken from the title of a 1912 book by William Walter Atkinson.

8 See discussion in Bowler, *Blessed*, 12.

never allowed anyone to discourage them. Heroes in these stories created their own identities and made their dreams come true.[9]

As previously mentioned, Pentecostals at first were very suspicious because that sort of thinking did not sound like the Bible, but rather like overconfidence, an opioid of optimism. But later Pentecostal preachers began to blur the line with a novel use of the word "faith." There was a seeming joining of forces between the New Thought and the New Testament as the mantra of "Believe in yourself" began to blur with the question, "Do you have enough faith?"[10]

Consider the ways that two aspects of Pentecostal thinking and theology contributed to this movement. The first is "words of faith." Pentecostals have a long and rich relationship between theology and orality. As a doctrine of creation, some Pentecostal theology emphasizes that words not only brought the universe into being in Genesis 1 but they also govern the world as an invisible force. Just as God was able to use his mind and his words in Genesis 1 to form and shape reality, everyone who is made in his image needs to speak their realities so that those realities may become true.[11] Pentecostals had always emphasized the importance of the power of speech dating back to their generally shared belief that speaking in tongues demonstrates the reality of spiritual power in their lives. In this context, words serve as a demonstration of the Holy Spirit's power, and from one perspective, that emphasis grew into these words of faith.[12]

---

9 For discussion of why late modernity provides the context for this thinking to flourish, see Anthony Giddens, *Modernity and Self-Identity: Self and Society in the Late Modern Age* (Stanford University Press, 1991).

10 See discussion in Bowler, *Blessed*, 14–15. One example Bowler highlights of this line blurring between secular and Pentecostal versions of the New Thought mantra comes from a pastor named E. W. Kenyon. Kenyon began to describe Christ's work and resurrection as a legal transaction that restored proper authority to believers. Before Christ died, Kenyon argued, Satan had authority over the world. But Christ's death and resurrection legally changed the legal status so that Christ had taken authority from Satan and had given it to believers. Thus, in Bowler's turn of phrase, the cross was "not a promise of things to come, but a guarantee of benefits already granted" (p. 17).

11 See the discussion of Kenyon on this point in Bowler, *Blessed*, 19.

12 According to Bowler and Reagan, "Within the setting of congregational

Faith is not simply an internal thing, but it needfully manifests itself in words so that it becomes real.[13] Bowler argues, "Words spoken in prayer, exorcism, worship, or plain conversation took on added weight, as Pentecostals cultivated a popular theology and practice of verbal power."[14]

A second key term is "the name of Jesus." In his book *The Wonderful Name of Jesus*, E. W. Kenyon taught that since the atonement transferred legal authority to the believer, the name of Jesus had forensic legal significance to everyone who used his name. Kenyon referenced John 14:14 to teach that prayer had a legally binding quality when believers used Jesus's name. "Asking" becomes a form of demanding, however, as believers claimed their spiritual rights by invoking the name of Jesus.[15]

---

worship, music served as a vehicle for the cultivation and transmission of the power of faith. This understanding of faith elevated the spoken word—in speech and in song—to new heights as the primary tool of unleashing God's divine blessing. As such, prosperity worship was neither simply affective as a harness for the right spiritual feeling nor merely pious entertainment for those seeking to attract new members—it was where song transformed faith into action, belief into power." Bowler and Reagan, "Bigger, Better, Louder," 208.

13 The turns of phrase used in these Pentecostal ideologies are widely familiar: if a Pentecostal person was feeling ill, she would not often not say that she "feels terrible," but will rather say that she is "healed in Jesus's name" and will "refuse to give the devil a foothold" by "claiming sickness." Bowler (*Blessed*, 145) cites Frederick Price's book *Is Healing For All?* and its "two short steps separated believers from divine health: (1) Prayer claiming God's promise of health; (2) thanksgiving and positive confession to be prayed 'until the physical manifestations of the healing takes place.'" Frederick Price, *Is Healing For All?* (Harrison House, 1976), 122.

14 Bowler, *Blessed*, 24. Interestingly, this is not terribly dissimilar to more progressive of Christian thought, such as Moltmann's theology of hope. In more psychologized Christian thought, the verbal is just as powerful, not for a supernaturality but for a radically interiorized spirituality.

15 Other Pentecostals built upon these insights. F. F. Bosworth wrote a book entitled *Christ the Healer*, first published in 1924 (with later editions appearing in 1948 and 1973), which contained "The Seven Redemptive Names of Jehovah." If a person was sick, he would call on Jehovah Rapha, the Lord who heals. If a person was fearful, she would call upon Jehovah Nisi, the Lord is our banner of protection. With these two realities, speech becomes reality and the name of Jesus becomes a form of invocation that functions as the previously described physical good luck charms.

After World War II, the movement grew, not only numerically, as a growing number of people were exposed to this teaching, but it also grew expectations for the benefits of faith to include creature comforts and conveniences. Many families considered purchasing previously unobtainable possessions, like homes, and considered filling those homes with amenities like indoor plumbing, telephones, and appliances.[16] The movement explained and artfully sailed in economic and cultural winds. That is to say, the prosperity gospel capitalized on the American economic growth of the 1950s by announcing that God was calling believers to greater economic prosperity. Prosperity gospel preachers proclaimed upward mobility to people who were already climbing the social and economic ladder during the boom years of the post-war American economy.[17]

During the 1950s, this movement continued to gain momentum from both the positivity of the New Thought movement and the power of Pentecostalism. From that first stream, Norman Vincent Peale influenced a generation by helping people maintain positive thinking. Several of his books are titled *A Guide to Confident Living* (1948), *The Power of Positive Thinking* (1952), and *You Can If You Think You Can* (1972). As may be inferred from these titles, Peale was convinced that God didn't want people to be skeptical of themselves but wanted each person to live life to the fullest by believing in himself or herself.[18] A second more Pentecostal

---

16 See Bowler, *Blessed*, 51.

17 Popular preachers of the time caught the public imagination. Kenneth Hagin taught his listeners about the Law of Faith, which taught that power had two domains: first, the legal domain—because Christ's victory transferred the rights of humanity from satanic possession to divine protection; and second, a scientific domain—because, Hagin argued, of the spiritual force of faith like the physical forces of gravity or electricity operated with causality. Spiritual forces could be wielded, and if a person does their part, God himself is obliged to fulfill his end. Oral Roberts also was influential to the movement, not by teaching unique principles, but by adopting mass media. He pioneered the widespread use of radio, television, and even educational schools among prosperity gospel evangelists. Because of his technological and educational initiative, Roberts was disproportionately influential.

18 Peale had his critics. Politician Adelai Stephenson famously opined, "I find Paul appealing and Peale appalling." Dave Hoekstra. "A Former President's

contribution of the 1950s was the Canadian "Latter Rain" revival.[19] This revival focused on healing, prophecy, and the restoration of biblical offices such as apostles, prophets, missionaries, pastors, and teachers. Its leaders taught that believers should claim a stronger measure of God's creative power as the true sons and daughters of heaven. Some critics have warned that these emphases represent a realized eschatology.[20]

During the 1960s and 1970s, believers were increasingly encouraged to expose themselves to God's Word.[21] Since God's Word is a powerful thing, the thinking went, then a believer should ensure that she exposes herself to a high quantity of biblical words by attending church, attending conferences, listening to sermon cassette tapes, wearing clothing featuring Bible verses, and purchasing décor displaying God's word around her house.[22]

There are two specific movements to note during the 1960s and 1970s. The first is the charismatic movement. Although the October 1965 cover of Time magazine rumored that God was dead,

---

Gag Order; Ford's Symposium Examines Humor in the Oval Office." *Chicago Sun-Times*, September 28, 1986. See also the recent book by Mark T. Mulder and Gerardo Martí, *The Glass Church: Robert H. Schuller, the Crystal Cathedral, and the Strain of Megachurch Ministry* (Rutgers University Press, 2020).

19 Scholars of the contemporary worship music (CWM) note the influence of this movement. The Latter Rain revival seems to be the first place which started to build a theology of worship from Ps 22:3, that "God is enthroned on the praises of his people." That, when we sing, praise creates the atmosphere in which God's manifest presence becomes more palpable and more direct. Thus, Christians encounter God through our music.

20 For a careful discussion of the eschatology of the prosperity gospel, especially the Latter Rain movement, see Michael J. McClymond, "Prosperity Already and Not Yet: An Eschatological Interpretation of the Health-and-Wealth Emphasis in the North American Pentecostal-Charismatic Movement," in *Perspectives in Pentecostal Eschatologies: World without End*, ed. Peter Althouse and Robby Waddell (Pickwick, 2010), 293–312.

21 See Bowler, *Blessed*, 65–66.

22 See Bowler, *Blessed*, 65ff. As a member in good standing with the Evangelical Theological Society and as an Associate Professor at The Southern Baptist Theological Seminary, let me hasten to affirm that God's Word is inerrant. It is "profitable for teaching, for reproof, for correction, and for training in righteousness" (1 Tim 3:16 ESV). But the Bible works spiritually and supernaturally, not superstitiously or magically. God's Word needs to renew our minds, shape our hearts, and direct our lives, not merely spruce up our walls or wardrobes.

a young generation was still looking for him, though not in their parents' churches.[23] Many younger people, especially in middle-class America, began to consider unusual approaches to religious life to access supernatural power by non-traditional means. This consideration took shape through the New Age movement, Transcendental Meditation, and even through recreational drug use. From alcoholism to the sexual revolution, this generation made well-documented attempts to encounter the transcendent in an attempt for healing and deliverance.

As a second movement, the 1960s and 1970s notably saw a proliferation of religious television. Christian television began broadcasting Sunday morning services by a handful of the nation's largest Protestant churches. What sort of churches could televise their services? Only churches that have the resources to not only purchase cameras and television equipment but also the sort of Sunday morning spectacle that would make for good television. Many of the churches that fit these descriptions were also proponents of prosperity teaching.[24] Through their broadcasting, these churches and their teaching gained national recognition as their excellent music, spectacular sanctuaries, and the mass communication style of their preaching made these churches destinations for pilgrimage. Eventually, these local broadcasts grew into different networks of Christian broadcasting with a disproportionate impact on the religious imaginations of America.[25] Because these services could be televised, many different Protestants, including Lutherans, Presbyterians, and even Roman Catholics, were able to watch these broadcasts and support these ministries without leaving their local church.[26]

Even after the scandals of televangelists of the 1970s, 1980s, and 1990s fractured the ministries of Jimmy Swaggart and Jim Bakker,

---

23 See the discussion in Bowler, *Blessed*, 69.

24 For a helpful list, see Bowler, *Blessed*, 75.

25 According to Bowler and Reagan, "Broadcasts were acts of mass spiritual persuasion, via the ebb and flow of emotion, as audiences were transfixed by sentiment more than doctrine. Particularly for those who taped their programs before live audiences, music became an indispensable tool for televangelism's ceaseless sentimentality." Bowler and Reagan, "Bigger, Better, Louder," 195.

26 See Bowler, *Blessed*, 76.

the televised influence of these churches spread, changing the expectations of average church attenders. Perhaps one of the explanations for the growth of the megachurch movement is that people, through their television viewing, began to expect a particular quality and style of preaching and a particular quality and style of music on a Sunday morning.[27]

A final point of discussion in our brief historical survey of the prosperity gospel and its related ideologies in recent American history should be the development of what Kate Bowler calls "soft prosperity."[28] The transition from classic prosperity teaching to soft prosperity, exemplified by the change from John Osteen to his son Joel, recognizes a change in emphasis, deemphasizing a causality between speech and physical success.[29] Soft prosperity ties psychological and physical success, believing that a rightly ordered mind leads, for example, to rightly ordered finances. The person with rightly ordered thinking will have a rightly ordered world.[30]

---

27 Bowler and Reagan state, "Prosperity preachers became the gatekeepers of television musical acts, and, in many ways, it was a perfect fit. The sweet theatricality of televangelism, coupled with its almost endless appetite to fill programming (particularly when programming expanded to twenty-four hours a day in the late 1970s) encouraged guest musicians to become a regular spectacle for millions of American viewers. Their back-to-back variety and talk shows had become the coveted openings for new and established artists and the era's most important popularizer of contemporary Christian musical acts." Bowler and Reagan, "Bigger, Better, Louder," 195.

28 Bowler, *Blessed*, 78, 110, 125–127.

29 In the words of Bowler and Reagen, "Leaders turned down the high emotional pitch and extreme promises that had characterized the previous decade in favor of feel-good messages of the postmodern turn toward therapeutic religion." Bowler and Reagan, "Bigger, Better, Louder," 190.

30 Soft prosperity explains why Paula White refers to herself as a life coach or motivational speaker and uses therapeutic language more often than invoking God's Word as a pastor or revivalist. Similarly, T. D. Jakes uses the language of therapy, with a message that centers on emotional healing. His best-selling book *Woman: Thou Art Loosed*, first published in 1994, focuses on psychological healing and addresses topics like domestic violence, discrimination, and divorce. That book and its attendant conferences moved Jakes into the national spotlight. Jakes continues to use therapeutic psychological categories in his preaching, often in ways that a previous generation of revival preachers or prosperity gospel teachers would have used sentimentality. This emphasis often expresses itself using the language and categories of self-care. While the previous generations

The Prosperity Gospel Defined

After this discussion of the popularity and history of the prosperity gospel-linked ideologies, we can more easily identify and define the prosperity gospel. There are four themes, four keywords, that Bowler uses to define and discuss the movement's beliefs of the prosperity gospel.[31] The first word is *faith*. For the prosperity gospel, faith is "an activator, a power that unleashes spiritual forces and turns spoken words into reality."[32] The next two words are very related: *wealth* and *health*. Faith is demonstrated in wealth and in health. Wealth and health are framed as realities that the spoken word becomes when it's accompanied by faith. A person's internal faith will be externalized, in wallets and bodies, in measurable ways so that material reality provides the means by which the success of immaterial faith can be evaluated.[33]

Then the fourth theme is *victory*. The prosperity gospel movement expects faith to be followed, or to be characterized by victory. As Bowler writes, "Believers trust that culture holds no political, social, or economic impediment to faith, and no circumstance can stop believers from living in total victory here on earth."[34] Faith is a demonstrable and observable pragmatic reality that leads to a successful and victorious life.

In order to better understand the context in which prosperity gospel churches use music, it is essential to recognize common liturgical practices of prosperity gospel churches. Bowler lists three: *confession, testimony,* and *tithing*. First, confession in the context of a prosperity gospel church generally is not the standard confession of sins familiar in many other Protestant traditions. Rather, such congregations might begin their worship services with positive confessions of health and wealth, such as "I am healthy and

---

of Pentecostals may have scoffed at this affirmative thinking, a new generation connected spiritual warfare with mental warfare and spiritual health with mental health. See discussion in Bowler, *Blessed*, 127.

31 These particular words form the structure of her book and provide her chapter titles.
32 Bowler, *Blessed*, 7.
33 See the discussion in Bowler, *Blessed*, 7.
34 Bowler, *Blessed*, 7.

wealthy, I am having good success."[35] Or, more subtly, "I am whole, I am complete, I have everything that I need."

A second liturgical practice, testimony, is unlike the testimony of traditional evangelical churches. Rather, the testimony meant here is that of divine provision where church attenders will testify of God's provision of a material benefit, such as a new car, a promotion or job, or even a new house. A third liturgical practice is tithing but, again, not in the context of the more familiar practices of offertory. Bowler writes, "Tithing eclipsed the sermon, worship, and communion as the emotional peak of the service, as pastors pushed their audiences to envision greater financial miracles."[36] A prosperity gospel church might use a traditional offering processional from the African American church but with heightened stakes. Again, Bowler cites an example from Detroit's "Perfecting Church," where recording artist and Pastor Marvin Winans "separated the givers from the bystanders when he asked those 'who give more than $30, but only more than $30' to stand and bring their offerings to the altar."[37]

This section has considered the popularity, the history, and the characteristics of the prosperity gospel. It has demonstrated how the combination of the positivity of New Thought and the power of Pentecostalism has ably navigated the cultural, economic, and religious currents of U.S. Christianity. The able navigation helps explain the broad cultural appeal of the movement and how it has been able to influence American evangelicalism. This influence, however, has not come without critics. And it is to those criticisms that we now turn.

Criticism of Prosperity Gospel Hymnody

There are many critics of the prosperity gospel and its wider theologies, ideologies, and practices.[38] Within this presentation's topic,

---

35 Bowler, *Blessed*, 128.
36 Bowler, *Blessed*, 128.
37 Bowler, *Blessed*, 128. Bowler cites Camilo José Vergara, *How the Other Half Worships* (Rutgers University Press), 153.
38 See David W. Jones and Russell S. Woodbridge, *Health, Wealth, and Happiness: Has the Prosperity Gospel Overshadowed the Gospel of Christ?* (Kregel,

however, I will focus particularly on criticisms from evangelical sources of the use by evangelical churches of the songs originating from the prosperity gospel movement. I use a video by Justin Peters and Todd Friel for many of my examples because of its popularity (2.5 million views), and the unusual clarity that these men bring to what for many believers is simply an instinctual "yuck." My research has identified five categories of criticism that by and large encapsulate the others.

I have labeled the first criticism as *problematic origins*. Critics argue that the songs related with the prosperity gospel are invalid because they originate from false churches. And, most specifically, their senior pastors (such as Hillsong's Brian Houston and Bethel's Bill Johnson). From this logic, the legitimacy of the songs is validated by the legitimacy of the church, which is validated by the qualifications of the Minister. So, the argument of problematic origins avers that a believer should not sing the songs because the songs come not from genuine churches but from false teachers.[39]

Related to and perhaps more basic, the second criticism could be generously labeled *doctrinal concern*. This is particularly a

---

2010); Costi W. Hinn, *God, Greed, and the (Prosperity) Gospel: How Truth Overwhelms a Life Built on Lies* (Zondervan, 2019); Kate Bowler, *Everything Happens for a Reason: And Other Lies I've Loved* (Random House, 2018); Russell P. Johnson, "The Gospel and the Prosperity Gospel: Joel Osteen's Your Best Life Now Reconsidered," *Theology* 121, no. 1 (January 2018): 28–34, doi:10.1177/0040571X17730980; Reed T. DeAngelis, Xiaohe Xu, and John P. Bartkowski, "Scriptural Coping: An Empirical Test of Hermeneutic Theory," *Journal for the Scientific Study of Religion* 58, no. 1 (March 2019): 174–191; Dieudonné Tamfu, "The Gods of the Prosperity Gospel: Unmasking American Idols in Africa," DesiringGod, 4 February 2020, https://www.desiringgod.org/articles/the-gods-of-the-prosperity-gospel.

39 A related common objection might be labeled *dangerous platform and networking*. Part of the problem is that prosperity gospel preachers do things with other prosperity gospel preachers. This is especially a criticism of Hillsong, which has a generous philosophy of cooperation. Their church hosts, or so the criticism goes, every well-known false teacher that "soils the landscape of evangelicalism today." Justin Peters and Todd Friel, "Why Your Church Shouldn't Play Bethel and Hillsong Music," Wretched, 8 February 2020, YouTube video, 21:53 (at 11:40), https://www.youtube.com/watch?v=Y0uFSYHVSRk. And by doing so, those in this category of objection claim, they have endorsed people like Bill Johnson, Kenneth Copeland, Joel Osteen, and Benny Hinn.

concern when speaking of Bethel Church. There are questions concerning Christology.[40] They claim prosperity gospel preachers hold that Jesus completely divested himself of his deity when he was on earth. Peters claims an aberrant teaching about the resurrection.[41] Of particular concern is Bethel Church's affirmation of "grave soaking."[42] Peters explains, "They believe that when one of their generals, … when they die, there's an anointing that resides on their bones and hence the grave. And if you go and lay on the tomb or lay on the grave, you can actually soak up this anointing from these dead people. That is straight out of the occult. That is demonic."[43]

A third related category of objection might be labeled *poor influence*. Here, the idea is that church attenders will read the copyright and author information, look up those names, and follow the rabbit trail into poor influence. They will discover that those songwriters are affiliated with particular churches and admire those churches. They will discover the names of the founders and pastors of those churches, admire them, and begin reading the books written by those pastors to the detriment of their faith.

A fourth criticism is the *emotionalism and romantic emphasis*.[44]

---

40 Critics such as Justin Peters argue that prosperity gospel preachers promote a "little gods" doctrine—that every human is a small god, similar to the criticism of Mormonism. Justin Peters, "Home," Justin Peters Ministries, https://justinpeters.org, accessed 30 January, 2022; see also, Peters, "Why Your Church Shouldn't Play."

41 According to Peters, "They believe that Jesus atoned for our sins down in hell where he literally had to be reborn. He died a spiritual death, ceased to be God, and had to be reborn. Jesus actually had to get saved. In fact, Bill Johnson says that Jesus was the first born-again man. This is a standard doctrine that Kenneth Copeland has taught for decades and Kenneth Haggen before him." Peters, "Why Your Church Shouldn't Play," 6:12. After quoting Bill Johnson as saying, "Jesus was the most normal Christian who ever lived," Peters draws out the conclusion, "And so if you're a Christian, then you are just like Jesus—all the rights, all the privileges."

42 To hear Bethel's perspective on this issue from Bill Johnson, see Bill Johnson, "Does Bethel Church Teach Grave Soaking? | Rediscover Bethel," Bethel, 24 June 2021, YouTube video, 25:54, https://youtu.be/Z8wBGmpOWR0.

43 Peters, "Why Your Church Shouldn't Play," 10:22. The leaders mentioned in this clip are Aimee Semple McPherson, Katherine Kuhlman, and Smith Wigglesworth.

44 A related concern is that the prosperity gospel only *appeals to the carnal*

While critics will admit that many individual songs do not contain poor theology, their criticism sharpens when discussing the intimate and personal imagery in the songs. Two Bethel songs are specifically named—"Closer" and "We Dance," which contains this bon mot: "When my faith gets tired and my hope seems lost, you spin me round and round and remind me of that song, the one you wrote for me, and we dance, we dance." The specific doctrinal criticism of this lyric is that it "borders on downright creepy."[45]

A fifth criticism might be labeled *financial support*. This criticism claims that if evangelical churches sing these songs in their church, by purchasing a license agreement through CCLI, orthodox churches flood heretical movements with finances. In the video, Todd Friel asked Justin Peters how much money is involved. Peters answered, "I couldn't even put a dollar sign on it. Multiple, multiple, tens of millions of dollars per year."[46] A quick visit to the CCLI website made this seem quite improbable.[47] But the dollar

---

appetite, rather than a spiritual one. Because of its universal appeal, attraction to the prosperity gospel doesn't require any supernaturally awakened spiritual appetite. According to Peters, "The prosperity Gospel appeals to universal human desires, the desire to be wealthy and the desire to be physically healed. Everybody on the planet wants that. They'll say if you come to Jesus, if you'll just ask Jesus into your heart, he'll make you rich, and you'll never have to be sick again. Well, there's seven billion people on the planet who want those things, and so they make this emotive response to the prosperity Gospel that's not the real gospel." Peters, "Why Your Church Shouldn't Play," 8:10. This seems to raise a valid concern. As the historical sketch above has shown, there are significant headwaters to the prosperity gospel that have their origins outside any distinctly spiritual or supernatural frames. I would, however, hasten to add that the desire to avoid eternal torture in hell could just as easily be conceived as universal. People surely have a shared instinct to avoid eternal pain. So insofar as this criticism implies that a true gospel requires a narrow appeal, at least in theory, further investigation dulls the critique.

45 Friel, "Why Your Church Shouldn't Play," 14:10.
46 Peters, "Why Your Church Shouldn't Play," 14:30
47 Christian Copyright Licensing International, "Church Copyright License®," accessed 30 January 2022, https://us.ccli.com/copyright-license. To be transparent, I regularly receive (small, but appreciated) royalty checks from CCLI. By comparison, Taylor Swift's album "Folklore" sold 1.6 million copies in 2020. And even if Ms. Swift charged $20 per album and did not pay Republic Records or its parent company, Universal Music, she would not have received multiple, multiple, tens of millions of dollars.

amount is not what is most important to Peters. Rather, he is concerned with the prospect of directly or indirectly offering financial support to what he considers a spiritually dangerous cause. His hypothetical illustration suggests,

> Let's just say that Planned Parenthood decides to write some Christian music that would pass a doctrinal smell test. Would you sing it in your church? Knowing that some money, every time you sing that song is going to an organization that murders babies, would you sing that song in your church? I would submit to you that singing Bethel and Hillsong, when you're sending money to those false churches, that's far worse.[48]

Response and a Way Forward

The concern I want to address for the remainder of this paper is that these various objections to evangelicals singing the songs from prosperity gospel churches stems from an unhealthy "liturgical scrupulosity." After some brief historical reflection, I propose three responses. In general, I fear these criticisms indicate a perhaps obsessive tendency that, in its pursuit of purity, has left the path of theologically robust and sustainable thinking. Critics proscribe particular songs, not because of the content of the song, but

---

48 Peters, "Why Your Church Shouldn't Play," 15:08–15:38. While I consider abortion murder and champion the ongoing defense of the unborn, I do not find Peters's hypothetical persuasive. A quick Google search reveals a list of corporations that *actually* donate money to Planned Parenthood, and I am unsure of how many Christian institutions or Christian leaders have consistently avoided all interactions with those corporations. Furthermore, the hypothetical scenario of a hypothetical worship song by an abortion clinic fails to account for the far greater overlap of beliefs and mission that exist between a prosperity gospel church and evangelical churches. Granting the significant theological divergences between them, evangelical Protestants and prosperity gospel songwriters share genuine common beliefs. This authentic overlap in beliefs makes for the genuine possibility of sharing cultural artifacts that promote a shared message. The illustration Peters offers only holds true to the extent that the songs produced by Hillsong and Bethel music are intended to be disingenuous and misleading. In Peters's hypothetical, there is no authentic reason for Planned Parenthood to create cultural artifacts with messages that could function in evangelical worship, other than financial gain.

because of the origin and association of the song. This logic indicates, to my mind, some unreflective and short-sighted tendencies in the Christian worship ecosystem.

Historical Reflection: Donatism, Relics, and Solomon's Song

In the desire to evaluate songs theologically, we ought to consider the vast theological treasures that doctrinal disputes of the past have given the church. Separatism is not the highest theology we have. Indeed, during the third and fourth-century persecution in the Roman Empire, many pastors were given the ultimatum to either renounce their faith or face punishment. As this season of persecution passed and Christianity became the official religion of the empire, churches had to consider what to do with pastors who had renounced their faith under persecution. And, more often, how to handle those people who were converted, baptized, or even ordained under the ministry of defecting pastors, or *traditores*. If a person was baptized by a pastor who renounced the faith, did he or she need to be re-baptized? The Donatist Party, a group of African opponents to Caecilian as bishop of Carthage because he was ordained by the traitor Felix, argued that the purity of the church is defended by the purity of its ministers. Thus, people who were baptized by someone who renounced the faith had an invalid baptism and must be re-baptized by a genuine pastor. This group of churches formed a purity movement that would not accept any believers into their churches who had not been baptized by one of their "pure" pastors. An imperial order in Carthage in the year 411 said, "No." The Catholic consensus that eventually prevailed was that the legitimacy of the ministry is not based upon the purity of its ministers. Nor is the legitimacy of a person's baptism based upon the piety of the person who baptized her.[49]

---

49 For the classic treatment, see W. H. C. Frend, *The Donatist Church* (Claredon, 1952) and T. D. Barnes, "The Beginnings of Donatism," *Journal of Theological Studies* 26, no. 1 (April 1975): 13–22. See also Gregg R. Allison, *Historical Theology: An Introduction to Christian Doctrine* (Zondervan, 2011), 619–621, 640. For those who might argue that Donatism was about sacraments, not songs, in many ways I completely agree. From this view, congregational songs are

Christian history, it must be said, has a long history of what might be called neo-Donatist renewals. The German Anabaptists, English Brownists (Barrowists), Plymouth Separatists, and even the Baptist Conservative Resurgence highlight a long list of people whose concern for the purity of the church has occasioned their withdrawal from more populous expressions of the faith. In calling for the rejection of Donatism, we must be careful not to concede to a logic that renders us as lowercase "donatists." Rather than arguing against separatism, precisianism, and primitivism, per se, this essay attempts to recognize the appeal toward purity and make the compelling case to engender a more catholic and thoughtful interaction as a greener pasture and better portion.[50]

Consider, for example, the overestimation of the initiative that church attendees possess. No churches of which I am aware forbid the singing of "It Is Well with My Soul" upon the fear that a church attender will read the copyright and author information, look up Horatio Spafford's affiliation with the "Overcomer" sect in Jerusalem, call married people to live celibate lives, and separate children from their parents.[51] Similarly, no churches that forbid the singing of Isaac Watts upon the fear that a church attender will read the copyright and author information, look up "Speculations on the Human Nature of the Logos," and be led into Arianism. An eight-point font copyright line on the final slide of a song which (might!) lead them to a website cannot have more cultural influence in a local church than the sermon, or the missions project, or the lifestyle of the church leaders. The point: churches interested in protecting their congregants from the heresy of the prosperity gospel

---

primarily didactic instruments rather than divine impartation of grace. To that argument, my response is the fallacy of *ad hominem*—the validity of the teaching or claim is nullified by the bias of the source. By referencing Donatism, however, I am not only addressing a common contemporary view of seeing songs as sacramental (see Jeremy Begbie, "Music, Mystery, and Sacrament" in *The Gestures of God: Explorations in Sacramentality*, ed. by Geoffrey Rowell and Christine Hall [Continuum, 2004], 173–91) but more so trying to address the strongest possible argument.

50 My thanks to Ryan Shelton for helping me clarify my thinking on this and many other points.

51 Jane Fletcher Geniesse, *American Priestess: The Extraordinary Story of Anna Spafford and the American Colony in Jerusalem* (Doubleday, 2008).

ought to labor to *repudiate heresy* rather than secondary affiliations. Churches interested in protecting their congregants from the culture of the prosperity gospel should ponder, for example, the average income of men that they promote as elders and church officers. The lifestyle of the people a church promotes within their ecclesiology is more influential than the publishing affiliations of their hymnody.

Almost every evangelical will easily admit that grave soaking is aberrant, misguided, and horrific. But historians of the church would remind people of several centuries of Christians doing similar aberrant, misguided, and horrific practices. During the long history of relic adoration, an index finger bone from John the Baptist or one of the three bodies of St. Matthew would draw Christians by the thousands, looking to see and to touch these items for spiritual benefit. As a Protestant heir of the Reformation, I condemn the practice and recommend John Calvin's *Treatise on Relics* as an underrated gem of Reformed piety (and comedy).[52] But as an appreciative reader of Augustine's *City of God* and Thomas Aquinas's *Summa Theolgiae*, I hesitate to label it occult or demonic.[53]

Concerning the emotional and romantic language of some of these songs, I readily admit that the song lyric does not translate well into spoken prose. However, there is a long history among Reformed Protestants, and especially among the Puritans like Samuel

---

52 According to Calvin, "With regard to the milk, there is not perhaps a town, a convent, or nunnery, where it is not shown in large or small quantities. Indeed, had the Virgin been a wet-nurse her whole life, or a dairy, she could not have produced more than is shown as hers in various parts. How they obtained all this milk they do not say, and it is superfluous here to remark that there is no foundation in the Gospels for these foolish and blasphemous extravagances." Calvin, *Treatise on Relics*, trans. Valerian Krasinski (Johnstone, Hunter & Co., 1870), 249.

53 Augustine states, "'This does not mean that the bodies of the departed are to be scorned and cast away, particularly the bodies of the righteous and faithful, of which the Spirit has made holy as instruments for good works of every kind. For if such things as a father's clothes, and his ring, are dear to their children in proportion to their affection for their parents, then the actual bodies are certainly not to be treated with contempt, since we wear them in a much closer and intimate way than any clothing." Augustine, *City of God*, trans. Henry Bettenson (Penguin, 2003) I.13, 22. See also idem, *The Confessions* IX.7; Thomas Aquinas *Summa Theolgiae* 3a.25.6.

Rutherford or John Cotton, interpreting the Song of Songs in ways that would blush the cheeks of many of my readers.[54]

Response 1: Primary Concern is Edification

The goal for all Christian worship services must be edification, and so, the highest priority for local church leaders choosing songs must be that they build up that particular people.[55] This priority renders as secondary questions like: Who sang these songs first? Who wrote them? Who recorded them? Church leaders must recognize their emerging role as hymnbook editors in the ecosystem of contemporary song choice. As such, they can learn from previous compilers of hymnals. Charles Spurgeon wrote in the preface to his hymnal, "A good hymn is not rejected by the character of its author, or the heresies of the church in whose hymnal it first occurred; so long as the language and the spirit commended the hymn to our heart, we included it, and believe we have enriched our collection thereby."[56] Similarly, John Rippon's supplement to Watts's *Psalms and Hymns* declares, "It has not been my Enquiry, *whose* Hymns shall I choose, but *what*, Hymns; and hence it will be seen that Churchmen and Dissenters, Watts and Tate, Wesley and Toplady, England and America sing Side by Side, and very often join in the same Triumph, using the same Words."[57] Secondary concerns, like

---

54 E.g., Rutherford writes, "O, what a fair One, what an only One, what an excellent, lovely, ravishing One is Jesus. Put the beauty of ten thousand thousand worlds of paradises, like the garden of Eden in one, put all trees, all flowers, all smells, all colors, all tastes, all joys, all sweetness, all loveliness, in one …. And yet it would be less to that fair and dearest Well-beloved Christ, than one drop of rain to the whole seas, rivers, lakes, and fountains of ten thousand earths." Samuel Rutherford, "Letter XXIX: To the Lady Kilconquilair," in *The Letters of Rev. Samuel Rutherford*, ed. Andrew Bonar (Oliphant Anderson and Ferrier, 1891), 95. Thanks to Ryan Shelton for the inspiration to track down this quote.

55 According to David Peterson, "The balance of Paul's teaching suggests that we view mutual ministry as the context in which to engage with God. Edification and worship are different sides of the same coin." Peterson, *Engaging with God: A Biblical Theology of Worship* (Eerdmans, 1993), 215.

56 As quoted in Christopher J. Ellis, *Gathering: A Spirituality and Theology of Worship in Free Church Tradition* (SCM, 2004), 167.

57 John Rippon, *A Selection of Hymns from the Best Authors, intended to be an appendix to Dr. Watts's Psalms and Hymns* (London, 1787), preface; cited in

original context, author, or tradition, only matter to the degree that they add or subtract from this first goal of edification.

Response 2: Most Relevant Context Is Local Context

A most relevant context for edification will be the local context. And the primacy of edification means that it is more important to avoid songs that cause distraction, rather than songs with unsavory origins. On occasion, it may be the case that a particular season, location, or proximity to a public scandal could make the origins of a song more prominent and, therefore, distracting. And such a distraction could hinder a song's usefulness for edification. When a song acquires a strong association to a particular event, person, or ministry, a congregation might think, "Wait a minute! That's a song by ____." A local church can always avoid a song that may have an unusually strong association that could cause a distraction, but the choice to avoid a song ought to be made because a known distraction could hinder edification in a particular context, not some ethereal standard of liturgical purity or spiritual taint from an unworthy author.

Let me provide an example to illustrate that what is distracting in one place is not distracting everywhere. I served as the dean of the chapel at Cornerstone University in Grand Rapids. One of the frequently sung songs in our chapel was "Your Love Is Strong" by Jon Foreman, the lead singer from Switchfoot.[58] The bridge of the song asks, "So why should I worry? Why should I freak out? You have all I need. You are all I need. Your love is, your love is strong." The song was well loved by the undergraduate students in Grand Rapids. It was useful for their spiritual edification. But I could not sing that song at my church in Minneapolis. When undergraduate students in Grand Rapids saw the lyric "Why should I freak out?" many of them thought, "Yeah! Why should I freak out? God has everything I need." But if I put that same lyric before the older, more conservative people of Bethlehem Baptist Church, they

---

Ellis, *Gathering*, 283n14.

58 Jon Foreman, "Your Love Is Strong," ©2008, Rubadub Publishing Publishing.

might actually freak out. We didn't sing that song in Minneapolis because it would have caused a distraction to that group of people that would have hindered its usefulness for edification.

It is easy to imagine that a worship pastor near Redding, California, whose congregation would be more likely to have strong negative associations toward a song by Bethel, could choose to avoid the song due to that distraction. The leaders of a local church may discern that such a distraction hinders a song's ability to edify their people and wisely decide to not sing it.

Response 3: Consider Varying Contexts

A third insight comes from ethnomusicologist Tia DeNora and her book *Music in Everyday Life*, and it is the call to consider the songs in varying contexts. Imagine a song that featured a heavy, percussive, rhythmic dance beat, with lyrics that said, "Move your body, Move your body, Get up and move your body." Now, if a conservative Christian person heard that song in the context of a club in, say, Miami, he might quickly want to leave that club. However, if he heard that same song in the context of the YMCA gymnasium in Louisville during a cardio-funk class, "Move your body, Get up and move your body" might be the sort of exhortation needed to get him through high-intensity aerobics.[59] The same song and lyric, performed in different contexts, has different inferences. In the club, it may mean something very sensual, while in the Y, it may simply mean "Hey, dad, get moving."

This is one of the powerful, beautiful, and dangerous aspects of music—a song can change its meaning upon different contextual hearings. The criticism that assigns essential meaning to a song because of its original context fails to appreciate a fundamental function of music as an artform.[60] The heresy of the prosperity

---

59 Denora describes excellent aerobic music as that "afford aerobic embodied agency, that enable the particular bodily movements, endurance, motivation, arousal and co-ordination, and that constrain the perception of fatigue." Tia DeNora, *Music in Everyday Life* (Cambridge University Press, 2000), 89.

60 For a lengthy discussion about the role of music meaning and ecclesial authority in the worship wars, see Anna Nekola, "Between This World and the Next: The Musical 'Worship Wars' and Evangelical Identity in the United States,

gospel withers outside its native context and evangelicals have an opportunity to engage in faith-filled subversive re-contextualization of songs in their faithful local church. There, a song once performed with professional production in palatial spaces can be re-contextualized with faithful, hobbyist volunteers in aging, baptist sanctuaries. Songs once promoted with attractive, charismatic, celebrity endorsements and slick marketing can be recontextualized with, well, evangelicals. Instead of the context projecting "the good life as young, beautiful, celebratory, and, of course, loud,"[61] Local churches subvert the prosperity gospel by contextualizing the songs with faithful expositional preaching, historic hymns, screaming infants, confession of sin and lament, meaningful church membership, church discipline, faithful volunteers, generosity toward missions, ministry to the aging and disabled, and strong doctrinal content.[62] You know, church.

1960–2005" (PhD diss., University of Wisconsin-Madison, 2008). This is not a kind of linguistic post-modernism denying authorial intent, but human works of art function differently than the words of Scripture with their divine author. In human works of art, intent can be discerned, but it is not necessarily directive.

61 Bowler and Reagan, "Bigger, Better, Louder," 211–212.

62 As an illustration, consider the widely seen video "How to Play Oceans on the Drums," Carlos Whittaker, 15 September 2014, YouTube video, 1:48, https://www.youtube.com/watch?v=POwayWGeQAU. If you are unfamiliar with it, it is a video of a local church's worship service featuring a female song leader playing the piano and singing the song, "Oceans." She is singing and playing piano with a light synth pad in the background at the slow tempo of approximately 64 beats per minute, when suddenly a drummer enters at a blistering 143 beats per minute, combining a heavy metal style double bass pedal with—what is even more inscrutable to the trained percussionist—felt mallets on an electric drum set. If you have seen the video, or you can imagine the scenario, you can believe me when I suggest that the woman leading the song has an entirely new appreciation for the lyric, "Where feet may fall." If you've ever played music in a public situation like this, you know that such occasions can inspire an entirely new depth of intercessory (or even imprecatory!) prayer. A bit of research on that video revealed that the gentleman playing the drums had come to faith in Christ shortly before the taping of that service, and had recently become a member of the music team. This would have been the context familiar to the entire church during that performance. Rather than a distracting train wreck of contradictory tempos, it seems to have been deeply appreciated by the grateful members of the local church. The performance means something quite different in that context than the millions of viewers watching this moment on YouTube.

Conclusion: Test Everything, Hold to What Is Good

Many of the criticisms warning evangelical churches from using the songs of the prosperity gospel movement are unwittingly liable to some of the same errors they critique. Critics are right to warn of superstitious tendencies within prosperity gospel churches. Sacred words, rituals, practices, and objects do not have magic power in themselves. And this means that neither are songs magically holy nor unholy based on their material associations. To maintain so would be to promote yet more superstition. Likewise, we should not allow financial concerns automatically to prevent the use of perfectly edifying songs for our congregations. Equating money with blessing automatically is a legitimate error of the prosperity gospel. In their eagerness to condemn these songs, some critics have ironically adopted the faulty logic of the prosperity preachers they criticize. Instead, churches ought to steward whatever resources they have available for the building up of their people.

Paul's exhortation in Romans 14 is especially instructive in this discussion. If someone offers a believer meat, they are to thank God for it and eat it. However, if that person says, "This food was served to an idol," they ought to refrain from eating out of a concern of causing the other weaker person to stumble. Consider a liturgical parallel. If a song goes up on the screen, a church should sing it. Yet we ought not to admire ministries that celebrate scandalous leaders nor parade the source of songs as if that were important. The apostle is especially concerned for believers who despise or pass judgment on each other. Paul writes, "Let not the one who eats despise the one who abstains, and let not the one who abstains pass judgment on the one who eats, for God has welcomed him. Who are you to pass judgment on the servant of another? It is before his own master that he stands or falls. And he will be upheld, for the Lord is able to make him stand" (Rom 14:2–4 ESV).

Christ is the cornerstone of the new temple that includes believers as living stones who are being built up into him. Everything a church does is for the upbuilding of the church. Because we are the temple, God's *building*, we need to *build* one another up. Because we are the *edifice* of God, we need to *edify* each other. Therefore, believers should not proscribe any of the tools that God, in his providence, provides for the task before us. And in all of these things, may we keep our eyes upon the Lord, who is able to make his church stand.

7

Possessions, Greed and the Christian Community: Interrogating the Prosperity Gospel in Africa in Light of Hebrews 13:1–6

Abeneazer G. Urga

THE GROWTH OF THE CHURCH in the continent of Africa is at an exciting stage. The current estimate is that by 2050 "forty percent of the world's Christian population will live in Sub-Saharan Africa."[1] The theological and missiological contribution within the continent and beyond has increased. Nevertheless, this exciting growth is not without its challenges. Ethnic conflicts, terrorism, natural disasters, corruption, poverty, the prosperity gospel, etc., have posed severe problems for the body of Christ on the continent. In this essay, I will raise the issue of the prosperity gospel in Africa and discuss why it is a problem and why it is making inroads within the continent. This discussion will then be followed by an explication of Hebrews 13:1–6 to address greed or "love of money" and provide three essential antidotes for the problem of the prosperity gospel in the African Christian community. The discussion of the passages will be situated in the author's discussion of possessions in exhorting the pilgrim people of God to persevere in the faith in the face of temptation, spiritual apathy, and persecution.

The Problem of the Prosperity Gospel

The prosperity gospel poses several problems among the Christian

---

1 Religion Media Centre, "Islam and Christianity Growing in Africa," 19 September 2019, https://religionmediacentre.org.uk/news/religion-in-africa-growing. See also David McClendon, "Sub-Saharan Africa Will Be Home to Growing Shares of the World's Christians and Muslims," Pew Research Center, 19 April 2017, https://www.pewresearch.org/fact-tank/2017/04/19/sub-saharan-africa-will-be-home-to-growing-shares-of-the-worlds-christians-and-muslims.

community in Africa. The undue emphasis on material success and the unquenchable thirst for more possessions have led many to the love of money and greed. The desire to obtain more wealth is not to support others who are in need but to fatten oneself with God's blessings. The mantra is not "bless me so that I can bless others" but "bless me so that I can be blessed." J. Lee Grady correctly notes that "the prosperity gospel … fuels greed because it focuses on getting and not giving."[2] Grady insists,

> At its core, [the prosperity gospel] is a selfish and materialistic faith with a thin Christian veneer. Church members are continually urged to sow financial seeds to reap bigger and bigger rewards. In Africa, entire conferences are dedicated to collecting offerings in order to achieve wealth. Preachers boast about how much they paid for suits, shoes, necklaces and watches. They tell their followers that spirituality is measured by whether they have a big house or a first-class ticket. When greed is preached from the pulpit, it spreads like a cancer in God's house.[3]

Such self-centered, greedy behavior does not have room for the mistreated, the poor or the stranger.[4] Hospitality to others and compassion to those who suffer in life do not have a place among those who propagate the prosperity gospel. Those who receive hospitality, love and welcoming gestures are those who have money and those who can sow financial seeds. The poor, the strangers and the afflicted are neglected because apparently, it is their mistake, for they lack the faith to get out of their misery. For the prosperity gospelers, "poverty … is defined as sin, laziness, and lack of faith. Human suffering is also perceived as a lack of Godly favour."[5]

---

    2 J. Lee Grady, "5 Ways the Prosperity Gospel Is Hurting Africa," Nairaland Forum, 23 September 2014, https://www.nairaland.com/1916135/5-ways-prosperity-gospel-hurting.
    3 Grady, "5 Ways the Prosperity Gospel Is Hurting Africa."
    4 Thinandavha D. Mashau and Mookgo S. Kgatle, "Prosperity Gospel and the Culture of Greed in Post-Colonial Africa: Constructing an Alternative African Christian Theology of Ubuntu," *Verbum et Ecclesia* 40, no. 2 (2019): 1.
    5 Mashau and Kgatle, "Prosperity Gospel and the Culture of Greed," 1.

With such a twisted theological excuse, the responsibility of the Christian community to care for one another and to show hospitality and compassion to others is abdicated. The emphasis is on self: individual success and abundance. Given the origin of the prosperity gospel, self-actualization, consumerism, and materialism as the main characteristics of the prosperity gospel are understandable.[6] The sad reality is that such self-advancement and narcissistic beliefs and practices are done at the expense of others.

Reasons for the Spread of the Prosperity Gospel in Africa

Thinandavha D. Mashau and Mookgo S. Kgatle denote that the "prosperity gospel found fertile soil in Africa."[7] However, what are the main reasons for the expansion of the prosperity gospel in Africa? Many of the critics of the prosperity gospel indicate how it is spreading, but they seldom indicate why this false teaching is blossoming in the continent. I believe there are two major reasons for the advancement of the practices and beliefs of the prosperity gospel.

First, the issue of poverty has a major role in the expansion of the prosperity gospel. Inadequate basic needs, lack of access to adequate healthcare and lack of a stable source of income to feed oneself or one's family force people to wholly depend on divine intervention. They hope either God or a certain supreme being will

---

6 Robert Wafawanaka, "The Bible, Power and Wealth in Africa: A Critique of the Prosperity Gospel in Sub-Saharan Africa," in *Navigating African Biblical Hermeneutics: Trends and Themes from Our Pots and Our Calabashes*, ed. Madipoane Masenya (Ngwan'a Mphahlele) and Kenneth N. Ngwa (Cambridge Scholars, 2018), 71.

7 Mashau and Kgatle, "Prosperity Gospel and the Culture of Greed," 2. Their statement that Africa is an ample context for the growth of the prosperity gospel is on point. Nonetheless, they exaggerate when they claim that the "prosperity gospel in Africa is synonymous with the Pentecostal–Charismatic Christianity." Similarly, on the previous page of their article, they state, "Christianity in post-colonial Africa is highly influenced and shaped by the prosperity message." These assertions deny the fact that there are millions of Christians and thousands of churches who do not hold to the teachings of the prosperity gospel. As such, these misleading statements should be rejected.

provide for their food, shelter, and clothing. In short, the poor and the needy in many contexts of Africa depend on the divine for their health and wealth. The prosperity gospel found this reality conducive to grow and exert its influence on the continent. Some might object to this argument by pointing out that there are a number of affluent and well-to-do Africans who have adopted the teachings and practices of the prosperity gospel. This is undeniable. But rich Africans who have succumbed to the prosperity gospel are also concerned that they might lose what they have. So their subscription to the prosperity gospel could be out of fear of poverty. To those who have a stable income, those who have access to sufficient medical care, and those who have a safety net or a credit card if they ever lack something to eat might not understand those on the other side of the ocean who are struggling to make ends meet and completely depend on divine provision or blessings if they are to provide for themselves and their families. While such an expectant position of many Africans is commendable, the prosperity gospel preachers have been exploiting this stance.

Second, many Western missionaries and, of course, a few Africans who have imbibed a dichotomistic theological framework and Enlightenment-influenced theology—both from the theological left and the theological right—have failed to address the whole person. Whether explicitly or implicitly, Enlightenment-influenced theology fails to acknowledge that the divine or the supernatural influences the physical or the visible world. In other words, many Western missionaries, for better or for worse, have emphasized that God only cares about people's souls and not their bodies. In so doing, they have created a great chasm between the body and the soul, which resulted in a disembodied theological anthropology. Unfortunately, this theological anthropology ruptured the typically African worldview, which traditionally considers man holistically rather than as a fragmented person. Such a teaching has forced many Africans to seek a solution in order to address their day-to-day reality. So, the question for Africans who have embraced Enlightenment theology or gospel is: does God care about our body? Does Jesus see our need for "our daily bread"? Does the Spirit care to save our bodies, our families, our cattle, our tribe, not just our souls?

Enlightenment theology and middle-class hermeneutics[8] are unable to answer these questions. Consequently, the prosperity gospel has benefitted both from the Enlightenment theology and middle-class hermeneutics. The dichotomy between the body and soul and the emphasis on escaping the earth and the body have given a slot to the prosperity gospelers to proclaim that health and wealth matter more than anything. What the prosperity preachers are doing is filling the gap that's lacking in Enlightenment-influenced theology proclaimed on the continent. Nonetheless, the prosperity teachings and practices ironically are also dichotomistic as the teaching elevates the material, the body, and the visible over the soul and the spiritual. Hence, the prosperity gospel should be rejected for the same reasons secularized evangelical theology and the middle-class hermeneutics that disembody the person should be rejected. The Epistle to the Hebrews provides us with three antidotes in countering the prosperity gospel in the African Christian community.

The Motif of Possessions and the Christian Community in Hebrews

The Epistle to the Hebrews discusses the concept of money, meaning either wealth or possessions. The notion is captured in various expressions: inheritance, wealth, reward, plunder, love of money, contentment with what one has, pay, blessing, give, share. The expressions are associated with both material and non-material/spiritual wealth and possessions.

In Hebrews 7:1–10, the author discusses how Abraham gave a tenth of his plunder to the King-Priest Melchizedek. Similarly, the Levites are to collect tithes from God's people. The author stresses that "Levi himself, who receives tithes, paid tithes through

---

8 One can observe a middle-class hermeneutic when an individual purely spiritualizes certain texts by interpreting them as if they only speak of the spiritual and not the physical and visible elements. For instance, when one takes the petition "Give us this day our daily bread" (Matt 6:11) as merely expressing asking for spiritual nourishment and not asking for food to eat, the person practices a middle-class hermeneutics. Such a tendency is not common among those who struggle to make ends meet but among well-to-do and middle-class individuals.

Abraham" (Heb 7:9).[9] Hebrews 10:32–39 details how the audience, upon their reception of the faith, experienced public shame, insult, and afflictions. They also took part in the afflictions of others. But in all these, they "endured a hard struggle with sufferings" (v. 32). They were sympathetic to others. They were willing to lose their earthly possessions, for they realized they "had a better possession and an abiding one" (v. 34). Holding onto the faith during severe hardships and their acceptance of letting go of their earthly possessions for the sake of the "better possession and an abiding one" has "a great reward." Hebrews 11:8 indicates Abraham's obedience to the divine call and that he trekked to the unknown "to receive an inheritance." Moses spurned the treasures of Egypt and chose to suffer for the sake of Christ (vv. 25–26). In Hebrews 13:1–6, the author urges the Christian community to avoid greed and be content with what they have. Again, the audience is exhorted to share with those who are in need of material possessions (v. 16). One cannot help but notice that there is a correlation between the Christian faith, perseverance and wealth or possessions in the Epistle.

The concern of the author in Hebrews is to encourage the Christian community to persevere and warn them of unfaithfulness who showed formidable faith in the face of persecution and suffering in the past. His intention is to help them "recall the former days" (10:32), fix their eyes upon Jesus (12:2) and repeat their past courageous stance, that is, embrace suffering by going to Jesus "outside the camp and bear[ing] the reproach he endured" (13:13). The author has detected that, unlike "the former days," the believers are tempted to give into pressure from outside. The "recipients ... appear to struggle with inhospitality, sexual immorality, greed, insubordination within their congregation and false teachings (Heb 13:1–17). Temptation, suffering, persecution and sin are threatening the spiritual and the physical well-being of the recipients."[10] As such, the author repeatedly warns them of the danger of

---

9 Unless otherwise noted, all Scripture quotations come from the ESV.

10 Abeneazer G. Urga, "The Background and Nature of Jesus' Intercession in Heaven as a High Priest for Believers in the Epistle to the Hebrews" (PhD diss., Columbia International University, 2021), 232.

apostasy and encourages them by pointing them to the better sacrifice, mediator, and Savior—the High Priest Jesus Christ. In Hebrews 13:1–6, the author continues to urge[11] the audience to live a godly life using a string of imperatival and hortatory statements. These exhortations provide us three main antidotes in resisting the prosperity gospel, which tilts the hearts of the Christian community in Africa to neglect brothers and sisters for the sake of self-gain, to be indifferent to those who are strangers and to those who are in need and to make material possessions the center of their lives. Now let us turn to the three antidotes to the prosperity gospel.

Brotherly Love

The author declares, Ἡ φιλαδελφία μενέτω. This first exhortation expressed with the present active imperative μενέτω indicates that brotherly love (φιλαδελφία) is a virtue that the Christian community must practice continually. The love among brothers and sisters is instituted by Jesus Christ who himself shared with humanity and "is not ashamed to call them brothers" (Heb 2:11; cf. 2:14).[12] Harold W. Attridge denotes that φιλαδελφία is uniquely a Christian expression that "[refers] primarily to the affection of natural siblings."[13] Craig R. Koester accentuates the practical nature of φιλαδελφία when he renders brotherly love as: "Let care for the brethren abide."[14] Φιλαδελφία is not an abstract concept but a practical care for those who are siblings in Christ. One of the many possible reasons that the author urges the audience to practice

---

11 The exhortations are conveyed using four imperative words: μενέτω (v. 1), ἐπιλανθάνεσθε (v. 2), μιμνῄσκεσθε (v. 3), and ἀρκούμενοι (v. 5)—a participle with the force of imperative.

12 Paul Ellingworth, *The Epistle to the Hebrews*, NIGTC (Eerdmans, 1993), 694; Craig R. Koester, *Hebrews: A New Translation with Introduction and Commentary*, AB 36 (Doubleday, 2001), 563.

13 Harold W. Attridge, *The Epistle to the Hebrews*, Hermeneia (Fortress, 1989), 385; cf. William L. Lane, *Hebrews 9–13*, WBC 47B (Word Books, 1991), 510.

14 Koester, *Hebrews*, 557; cf. 563.

φιλαδελφία is because "some have forsaken (ἐγκαταλείπω) Christian fellowship."[15]

Unlike the former days, they are afraid of losing their possessions and of going through taunts, afflictions and humiliations for the sake of the faith. Personal preservation contradicts practicing brotherly love. Selfishness and the neglect of fellowship are antithetical to care for brothers and sisters in practical ways.

The prosperity gospel in Africa has made a dent on genuine fellowship among Christian brothers and sisters. It has been a barrier in practicing φιλαδελφία. The theology of the prosperity gospel denies that there is suffering and difficulty in the Christian pilgrimage. And if a Christian suffers because of his or her faith, it is because he or she lacks faith. Those who have embraced such a teaching either attempt to convince suffering Christians to embrace a pain-free, suffering-free, prosperous, and gleeful life on earth or they abandon fellowshipping with and caring for suffering Christian brothers and sisters, leaving the suffering saints to their own demise.

On the contrary, the exhortation to "let brotherly love continue" compels Christians—in this case, Christian Africans—to care for their brothers and sisters continually. The expression μενέτω, as Attridge correctly points out, is "a catchword link" echoing Hebrews 6:10, 10:24, and 10:32, where the audience is encouraged to serve Christian brothers and sisters continually and remain faithful to Christ.[16]

One vital passage that sheds light on what brotherly love entails is Hebrews 13:16. It reads, "Do not neglect to do good and to share what you have, for such sacrifices are pleasing to God." The Christian community the author addresses is expected to offer sacrifices. In Hebrews 13:15, Christians are to offer a sacrifice of praise continually. But Hebrews 13:16 provides good deeds and sharing as another sacrificial offering with which God is pleased.

---

15 Urga, "The Background and Nature," 311–312.
16 Attridge, *The Epistle to the Hebrews*, 385.

The hapax legomenon εὐποιΐα conveys the idea of "acts of kindness"[17] or "concrete acts of mutual concern."[18] Similarly, κοινωνία allows the Christian community to practice brotherly love. Scholars rightly note the affinity between εὐποιΐα and κοινωνία. Some even entertain the idea that the terms are a hendiadys.[19] Christians are urged not to neglect doing good for one another or sharing material possessions or wealth with those who are in need.[20] Lane postulates that "The financial connotations of the term κοινωνία have been widely recognized .... Partnership with other believers carried economic overtones."[21] Hans-Friedrich Weiß clearly sees the connection between Hebrews 13:1 and Hebrews 13:16 because εὐποιΐα corresponds with the term κοινωνία. Weiß states, "εὐποιΐα denotes 'doing good,' 'charity' in the broadest sense, not just caring for the poor in the community."[22]

The necessity to care for other brothers and sisters stems from the reality that the Christian life here on earth is not free of suffering. Nonetheless, brotherly love demonstrated through sharing, caring and fellowship enables Christians to persevere in the face of persecution and suffering.

In short, brotherly love through the act of kindness and sharing what one has is an essential antidote to the self-obsessive, narcissistic and individualistic teachings of the prosperity gospel. Brotherly love is deeply caring, practical, sacrificial and communal.

Hospitality to Strangers

The author of Hebrews offers a second exhortation to his audience: "Do not neglect to show hospitality to strangers" (Heb 13:2).

---

17 Lane, *Hebrews 9–13*, 552; Koester, *Hebrews*, 572.
18 Attridge, *The Epistle to the Hebrews*, 401.
19 Ellingworth, *The Epistle to the Hebrews*, 721.
20 David G. Peterson, *Hebrews*, TNTC (IVP Academic, 2020), 325.
21 Lane, *Hebrews 9–13*, 552; cf. Thomas R. Schreiner, *A Commentary on Hebrews*, Biblical Theology for Christian Proclamation (B&H, 2015), 424.
22 Hans-Friedrich Weiß, *Der Brief an die Hebräer*, KEK (Vandenhoeck und Ruprecht, 1991), 742, "Neben κοινωνία bezeichnet εὐποιΐα das 'Tun des Guten,' die 'Wohltätigkeit' im weitesten Sinne, nicht also nur die Fürsorge für die Armen in der Gemeinde."

The practice of hospitality was considered a virtue in antiquity. Hence, hospitality is not a uniquely Christian virtue. Gustav Stählin denotes that "In times of persecution, such as those underlying Hb. and 1 Pt., hospitality to refugees and exiles was most important."[23] Indeed, as we have pointed out earlier, sufferings and persecution are the realities of the audience's journey in the faith. Therefore, the exhortation could be urging Christians to care for those who are ostracized, forced to migrate or lost their possessions and wealth for the sake of their faith. Many commentators suggest that the command to care for strangers is only concerned with fellow Christians.[24] However, the exhortation to show hospitality to strangers is inclusive of both fellow-believers and unbelievers.[25]

It was the custom of the early church to receive itinerant teachers, apostles and prophets or anyone who came in the name of the Lord (Did. 11–12). The Didache specifically urges believers, Πᾶς δὲ ὁ ἐρχόμενος ἐν ὀνόματι Κυρίου δεχθήτω ("But everyone who comes in the name of the Lord must be received"; Did. 12.1). The term δεχθήτω is an imperative directed to believers to be hospitable to others for the sake of the Lord's name. A similar notion is conveyed in Romans 12:13, 1 Peter 4:9, and 3 John 5–8. These passages make clear that Christians are to "[offer] travelers lodging and something to eat and drink (Acts 10:23; 21:16; 28:7)."[26]

Hospitality to strangers, as argued earlier, includes those outside of the fold of the faith.[27] Christians are to show care for those in need by welcoming strangers—whether believers or unbelievers—into their houses and providing food and drink. But this hospitality to strangers is not to be confined to their houses, for the audience is also urged to "remember those who are in prison" (Heb 13:3); in other words, they were to go to those who could not appear at the doorstep of the Christians' households. Believers are to

---

23 Gustav Stählin, "... φιλοξενία, φιλόξενος," in *TDNT* 5:21.

24 Ellingworth, *The Epistle to the Hebrews*, 694; Stählin, "... φιλοξενία, φιλόξενος," in *TDNT* 5:21; Schreiner, *A Commentary on Hebrews*, 411; Gareth L. Cockerill, *Hebrews*, NICNT (Eerdmans, 2012), 679–681; Michael J. Kruger, *Hebrews for You* (Good Book, 2021), 216–217.

25 Peterson, *Hebrews*, 315.

26 Koester, *Hebrews*, 563.

27 Koester, *Hebrews*, 563.

go to those who are mistreated. In the past, they had identified with Christian brothers and sisters in prison. They had shown compassion and partnered with Christians who suffered for the sake of the faith (Heb 10:33–34). It is possible that the author had noticed indifference and lack of care for those who were in prison. Spiritual apathy, self-preservation, shame and selfishness could have been the reasons for the neglect of Christian prisoners.[28] Whatever the reason, the community is commanded to demonstrate their care, empathy and compassion to the mistreated. They were to act as if they themselves were incarcerated with those who were languishing in prison.

Both receiving strangers and remembering mistreated prisoners are costly. Christians who are involved in such ministries sacrifice money, time and space in entertaining strangers and others who are in need. Michael Kruger captures the essence of hospitality when he posits:

> In our day we easily confuse biblical hospitality with entertaining. Hospitality is not just about hosting dinner parties. It is more other-centered. It focuses on meeting a need rather than on having an enjoyable time. The motive is different.[29]

Such sacrificial hospitality and attentiveness to those in need is a thorn in the flesh of the inflated theology of the prosperity gospel. Christian hospitality's focus on others rather than on self, the emphasis on sharing with those who could not repay or give back a hundredfold, and the distribution or sharing of wealth and possessions to meet the needs of others rather than the accretion of wealth help counter the practices and beliefs of the prosperity gospel. Genuine hospitality deters the unhealthy fixation of some Christian Africans on self-infatuation, greed and an insatiable appetite for wealth and prosperity.

---

28 Schreiner, *A Commentary on Hebrews*, 412.
29 Kruger, *Hebrews for You*, 217.

Do Not Love Money, but Trust the Lord

A third exhortation that helps the contemporary church in Africa to resist the prosperity gospel is the author's exhortation to the audience, "Keep your life free from love of money, and be content with what you have" (Heb 13:5). Note that the author employs here the adjective ἀφιλάργυρος. The expression ἀφιλάργυρος ὁ τρόπος here exhorts the audience not to love money or be greedy, whereas φιλαδελφία and φιλοξενία urge the audience to practice brotherly love and to love the stranger (or literally "hospitality"). As in the former days, there is the possibility that persecution might occur and that the audience could be subjected to the plundering of their property (Heb 10:34). As such, the amassing of wealth is not going to be the solution.[30] Lane opines that "the frightening prospect of renewed suffering … may have encompassed the members of the house church to seek to secure their future through the accumulation of material resources."[31] However, such a disposition is contrary to practicing brotherly love and hospitality. Above all, the love of money or greed contradicts trusting the Lord. Greed is an expression of utter selfishness[32] and outright distrust of the Lord's help. Perhaps the oft-quoted Pauline passage can explain what the love of money does to Christians:

> But those who desire to be rich fall into temptation, into a snare, into many senseless and harmful desires that plunge people into ruin and destruction. For the love of money is a root of all kinds of evils. It is through this craving that some have wandered away from the faith and pierced themselves with many pangs. (1 Tim 6:9–10)

Greed is behind the curtain of every single evil. Those who want more wealth and those who love money are falling behind and becoming negligent of their Christian duty: loving their brothers

---

30 Ellingworth, *The Epistle to the Hebrews*, 698.
31 Lane, *Hebrews*, 2:518.
32 Filson, F. V. *'Yesterday': A Study of Hebrews in the Light of Chapter 13* (SCM, 1967), 79.

and sisters in need, being hospitable to strangers, and attending to those suffering, because they are in a rush to secure more wealth and save their own skin from impending persecution.

The audience, instead, is urged to be content with what they have. The struggle to have more ought to be replaced with trusting the Lord for provision. The author provides two reasons for the audience to trust the Lord and be content with what they have. First, God promised, "I will never leave you nor forsake you" (Heb 13:5; cf. Deut 31:6, 8; Josh 1:5). The second reason is another Old Testament quotation: "The Lord is my helper, I will not fear; what can man do to me?" (Heb 13:6; cf. Ps 118:6). The Lord's constant presence around his people allows the audience to confidently declare that the Lord is their helper and is providing for what they need. If and when persecution arises, they will be able to face it joyfully and without fear of men.

Conclusion

The prosperity gospel preachers demand from the people more money, more seeds, more wealth so that they can have more cars, additional planes, numerous houses, etc. Their congregants pour their money and goods out to meet these non-stop, avaricious, and selfish quests. The preachers' love for money has blinded them so that they fail to extend care to their brothers and sisters in the pew who are hoping to get out of the cycle of poverty, to pay their next month's rent, send their kids to school, or pay their medical bills. In the quest for more suits for the following week's conference, the prosperity gospel teachers have denied strangers food, drink, clothing or a place to stay. They practice inhospitality and constantly neglect those suffering for the faith. This error could be corrected if and when Christian Africans take heed of the exhortation to be content with what they have and trust the Lord for provision and help in the time of their need rather than calculating to amass material wealth.

8

Conceptions of the Good Life in the Apostolic Era

Todd A. Scacewater

How did Jesus and the apostles conceive of "the good life," or perhaps to use more biblical terminology, "blessing" or "happiness?" Broadly speaking, prosperity teaching assumes that "blessing" primarily consists of wealth and perhaps also health (hence the phrase "health and wealth gospel"). One way to consider whether this assumption is correct is to analyze the biblical passages that talk about blessing and happiness to see how and to what extent health and wealth are related. Another way might be to examine the saints of the Old and New Testaments to see whether they were rich and healthy. These two approaches might give some data in favor of prosperity teaching while also providing some conflicting evidence. But another, more historically and culturally sensitive approach is to consider ways in which these terms were spoken and written about by those of the same time and culture as the biblical authors. Such an inquiry would give us a more methodologically sound starting point for beginning a study of the biblical authors' understanding of these concepts.

Behind such an approach to investigating the meaning of biblical concepts is what I would consider a hermeneutical axiom, that successful communication will use words and refer to concepts in ways that are typical for the language and culture of the audience. If one were to use such concepts in ways that differed greatly from typical usage, miscommunication would occur, and the audience would not understand the intent of the author. Speakers take this aspect of communication into account when they use language, at least to the extent that they want to be understood by their audience.[1] My assumption is not that biblical authors can use a word or concept only in the same way that their non-Christian contemporaries used them. Rather, my assumption is that knowing the variety of ways that non-biblical authors thought about blessing and happiness will give us a contextual background *against which to test our theories* of how biblical authors from the same era employed these concepts in their discourse.

In this essay, I limit my scope to the New Testament era and will engage only with Greek literature, mainly the Greek philosophers, playwrights, historians, and commoners. I will begin by surveying the variety of terms used for the concepts "blessing" and "happiness" in Greek literature. Next, I will consider the ways that Greek commoners and authors defined these concepts. Third, I will survey how Greek authors construed the relationship between virtue, external goods, and happiness. Finally, I will conclude with some reflections on how this data helps us better understand what Jesus and the apostles meant when they referred to the concepts of blessing and happiness. My use of English terminology will be somewhat fluid throughout the essay, using "happiness," "blessedness," and "the good life" as basically synonymous terms that refer to the concept "the good life."

Lexical Abundance in Happiness Discourse

Discussions about "happiness" among the Greeks usually focuses on the lexeme εὐδαιμονία, perhaps because the lexeme is used commonly throughout academic literature and because it is the technical term on which Aristotle focuses in his *Nicomachean Ethics*. The prefix ευ- signifies "good," while δαίμων signifies the power that controls one's fate or soul. But this lexeme is only one of many that is used to refer to the good life in Greek literature. Several terms employ the ευ- prefix ("good, well"), such as εὐζωέω, "I live well," εὐπραγία (Ion. εὐπρηγίη), "good conduct, well-being,

---

[1] What I have stated as a hermeneutical axiom is a rough, simplified version of what is called the Communicative Principle of Relevance, one of the two fundamental principles of Relevance Theory. See Dan Sperber and Deirdre Wilson, *Relevance: Communication and Cognition*, 2nd ed. (Blackwell, 1995).

success," εὖ πρήσσοντα, "doing well," εὐτυχέω, "I prosper" (adj. εὐτυχής, noun εὐτυχία), εὔμοιρος, "well-endowed by fortune" (μοῖραν = "lot, destiny"), εὔρουν, "flowing well" (used by the Stoics, ῥόος /ῥοῦς = "stream, flow of water, current"), and εὐπαθέω, "I make glad."[2]

In addition to words with the ευ- prefix are others such as ὄλβιος, "happy, blessed," ἀρκέω in the passive, "be satisfied with," μακαρίζω (adj. μακάριος), "I bless, I am blessed," and τὸν ἀγαπητότατον βίον, "most beloved life." Greek authors also employ a number of antonyms to refer to the unfortunate or unhappy, such as δυστυχέω (adj. δυστυχής), "I am unfortunate, unlucky," δύστηνος, "wretched, unhappy," and τλήμων, "suffering, unhappiness." Other terms such as κακόω, "I harm, mistreat" and σχετλιάζω, "I complain, grumble," are related to the state of unhappiness.

This list of terms is not comprehensive but is fairly representative of the abundance of lexical options available in Greek happiness discourse. From this data, we should conclude, first, that we ought not limit our attention to discussions of εὐδαιμονία when we ask what the Greeks understood by the good life. Second, this lexical abundance might lead us to believe that the Greeks were especially interested in discovering the means to the good life. When speakers of a language employ more than a dozen lexemes to refer to different facets of a concept (or its opposite), we might conclude that the concept is both commonly discussed and sufficiently complex enough to demand such a lexical repertoire.

Definitions of Happiness

When considering ancient Greek perceptions of what constitutes happiness, we can divide the sources into philosophers, playwrights, historians, and commoners. Beginning with commoners, we can only infer their understanding of happiness from literary sources. Aristotle wrote that most people defined happiness (εὐδαιμονία) as "living well and doing well" (τὸ δ' εὖ ζῆν καὶ τὸ εὖ πράττειν; *Eth. nic.* 1095a). He further explained that most

---

[2] These glosses are taken from LSJ.

common men equate living well to having some sort of good such as health, honor, pleasure, or wealth. This conception of happiness occurs frequently in the playwrights, who employ happiness language for those who have many honorable children, possess good land and fortune, or have an occasion to celebrate.[3] They could also speak of external "good things" (ἀγαθῶν), which imply that one would be happy or living the good life.[4] The playwrights likely reflect the views of commoners since their plays were written and performed for their entertainment.

Among the historians, Herodotus relates an account of the Athenian law-giver Solon, which recurs often in later writings and seems to have influenced many people's views on happiness.[5] Croesus, king of Lydia, asked Solon who is the happiest (ὄλβιος) person he has met in his travels (*Hist.* 1.30). Solon replies that Tellus of Athens was the happiest he knew because his country was good, he saw his grandchildren, and he died an honorable death on the battlefield. Second happiest was the mother of Cleobis and Bito; she was so honored by her children that she was considered blessed (μακαρίζω). So, Solon judged happiness by external circumstances such as health, honor, and a thriving society, but not necessarily wealth. Croesus is insulted and asks whether his happiness (εὐδαιμονία) is so little in Solon's eyes, demonstrating the king's hedonistic conception of happiness. The statesman responds that, while the king is wealthy, he has not yet died, so fortune may still strip him of all his external goods. So for now he should be called fortunate (εὐτυχής), but not happy (ὄλβιος). Summarized later by Ausonius, Solon's claim was "we must behold the end of life first: then we can judge—if prosperity [*felicitas*] abides."[6] Happiness,

---

[3] Euripides, *Ion* 560–569; *Tro.* 325, 510; *Phoen.* 424; Aristophanes, *Plut.* 629, 655.

[4] Aristophanes, *Av.* 587–588.

[5] Plutarch, *Comp. Sol. Publ.* 1; Aristotle, *Eth. nic.* 1100a; Ausonius, *Masque of the Seven Sages* 91–106; Dio Chrysostom, *Fel.* 2.5; Diog. Laert. 1.50. Diogenes relates the question put to Solon, summarizes his answer, and says Solon "went on in words too familiar to be quoted here." The editor of the Dio Chrysostom LCL volume cited here says this tale of Solon and Croesus is "one of the most famous tales in Herodotus" (LCL 385: 49 n. 6).

[6] Ausonius, *Masque of the Seven Sages* 103–104.

then, is an abiding state, something permanent that cannot be stripped away through misfortune. While Herodotus records the story, his own conception of happiness seems to differ and focus more on wealth and prosperity, considering his own use of ευδαιμ- lexemes (e.g., *Hist.* 1.5, 133, 196; 3.14, 52; 5.8, 31).

Among the philosophers, we can consider the various conceptions from Socrates through the Stoics, including their dialogue partners. In *Crito*, Socrates equates "living well" with living "nobly and justly" (Plato, *Crito* 28b). How can one live nobly and justly? They can do so if they have "many good things" (πολλὰ κἀγαθὰ), the ultimate good being wisdom (Plato, *Euthyd.* 279–283). His desire for wisdom as "a good" is evident at the end of *Euthyphro*, where he regrets not learning anything positive about the definition of piety, for if he had, he would have "lived a better life" (Plato, *Euthyphr.* 16a). That pursuit of more wisdom is evident also at the end of the *Apology*, where he admits that he is not as wise as the gods, and so he is still striving for more wisdom for himself and others (Plato, *Ap.* 23). B. Silver notes that Socrates certainly believes he is living the good life, since "living well and nobly and justly are the same" (*Crito* 28b) and he is acting justly by not escaping his execution.[7] So Socrates's view of happiness is that it is a certain kind of living that attains wisdom and constantly pursues more of it.

Plato's considerations of happiness are more metaphysical. He spoke of happiness as the soul being "made glad" (εὐπαθέω) upon beholding the forms, that is, true reality (*Phaedr.* 247d). All souls must behold this true reality before being born, otherwise the perception of reality would never be possible for humans. In this preexistent state, souls are ὁλόκληρα δὲ καὶ ἁπλᾶ καὶ ἀτρεμῆ καὶ εὐδαίμονα φάσματα ("complete and simple and calm and happy apparitions"). Once the soul is incarnated, Plato asserts,

> If now the better elements of the mind, which lead to a well ordered life and to philosophy, prevail, they live a life of happiness and harmony here on earth, self controlled and orderly,

---

7 Bruce Silver, *Philosophy as Frustration: Happiness Found and Feigned from Greek Antiquity to the Present*, Studies in Moral Philosophy 5 (Brill, 2013), 17–42.

holding in subjection that which causes evil in the soul and giving freedom to that which makes for virtue. (*Phaedr.* 256a–b)[8]

This use of the intellectual virtues to behold true reality is the highest good, but there are also lower goods. Seeking in *Philebus* to counter the thesis that pleasure is the ultimate good, he points out that pleasure is often mixed with pain and that pleasure does not always (or often) share in truth, beauty, or symmetry. So pleasure cannot be the chief good, but at the same time, one would not want wisdom or dialectic without any pleasure whatsoever. So "we should seek the good, not in the unmixed life but in the mixed" (*Phileb.* 60e–61b). The key is in the proper priorities: "mind is ten thousand times nearer and more akin to the nature of the conqueror than pleasure" (*Phileb.* 67a).

Aristotle was more holistic and pragmatic in his considerations of happiness than his predecessors. Employing εὐδαιμονία as a technical term in his *Nicomachean Ethics* and his *Politics*, he described the concept in-depth and defined it as "activities in conformity with virtue" (*Eth. nic.* 1100b). Since εὐδαιμονία is the end (*telos*) of man (*Eth. nic.* 1097a–b), we are happy when we live according to our end. Many rightly translate Aristotle's εὐδαιμονία as "flourishing" rather than "happiness" because the former implies activity, whereas "happiness" implies a state. Aristotle was clear that he thought the happy person was the one practicing virtue, not simply possessing it passively (*Eth. nic.* 1098b–1099a). Contrasting with some strands of Greek thought, Aristotle noted that flourishing cannot be achieved universally if it is given by the gods, since they are whimsical. Rather, man must attain happiness through human effort in accord with virtue (*Eth. nic.* 1099b).

Happiness is not only the ultimate good of man, but even more so of the community. Man is a "political animal" (*Pol.* 1253a; *Eth. nic.* 1097b, 1162a, 1169a), so the good of the nation is "nobler and more divine" than that of an individual (*Eth. nic.* 1094a). Since flourishing is the activity of virtue, politics (πολιτική) should be viewed as the study of the social conditions required for fostering the virtuous life (*Eth. nic.* 1094a). Thus, Aristotle's theory of the

---

[8] Translation in LCL 36: 501.

good life included both the individual and his or her cultivation of virtue as well as the social conditions required for actively employing such virtue. His theory is probably the most social from the thinkers of this era.

While Socrates, Plato, and Aristotle influenced many of the Greek philosophers, the Stoics did as well. Their conception was teleological like Aristotle's, and they also considered virtue to be man's end. However, their conception of virtue differed. While Aristotle understood virtue as the mean between two vices, the one of excess and the other of deficiency (*Eth. nic.* 1106b–1107a), the Stoics understood virtue as conformity to nature and detachment from worldly concerns. Epictetus equated virtue with "the good," which includes at least the intellectual virtues of intelligence, knowledge, and right reason (*Diatr.* 2.8). Active virtue for Marcus Aurelius could mean treating every act as if it were one's last, with reason and simple dignity, apart from self-love and carelessness (*M. Antonius Imperator Ad Se Ipsum* 2.5). Likewise, if a man accepts the destiny that nature spins for him and does his duty according to justice, then he will come to the *telos* of life, to which he must come "pure, peaceful, ready for release, needing no force to bring him into accord with his lot."[9] In another place, Aurelius says the person who is fortunate (εὔμοιρος) has a good disposition of the soul, good emotions, and good actions (*Med.* 5.36).

The result of living by this Stoic conception of virtue was the good life, for which the Stoics used a number of terms. Apart from the typical εὐδαιμονία were also ἀπάθεια ("freedom from emotion," "tranquility") and εὔρουν / εὔροια ("flowing freely, prosperous") that is, not being perturbed by externals.[10] The Stoics used these two terms frequently, but Epictetus also used others in parallel with these, such as freedom (ἐλευθέριος), calmness (ἀταραξία) being fortunate (εὐτυχέω), and εὐδαιμονία (*Diatr.* 1.4; 1.28; 2.18).[11] Marcus Aurelius wrote of virtue enabling one to live "a free-flowing

---

9 Translation in LCL 58: 65.

10 Philostratus of Athens used the word to refer to the inability to breathe "smoothly" or "fluently" because their innards are cramped (*Gymn.* 30).

11 Plotinus in the third century took ἀταραξία to be the Stoics' central characteristic of the good life (*Enn.* 1.4.1).

and pious life" (δύναται εὕρουν καὶ θεουδῆ βιῶσαι βίον; *M. Antonius Imperator Ad Se Ipsum* 2.5).

In sum, the concept of happiness, blessedness, or the good life is understood variously, but some main strands of thought can be determined. The common people understood happiness to consist mostly in prosperity. The statesman Solon deprecated wealth as a primary good and famously claimed that temporal fortune can always be stripped away. Nevertheless, he still considered happiness to consist in certain external goods. Herodotus used happiness language in accord with the ideas of the common people perhaps because historians tend to focus on "history makers" and powerful societies, whose wealth and prosperity comes bundled with their historical rise to fame. The philosophers, though, viewed happiness teleologically, as the goal of our nature. Virtue is the primary means by which to achieve happiness, even if virtue is defined differently. Plato and the Stoics emphasized the ordered life, while Socrates and Aristotle emphasized the active pursuit or use of virtue. None of the philosophers viewed wealth as a necessary condition for happiness, although some of them did leave a role for certain external goods other than virtue, which we may now consider.

Virtue, Externals, and Happiness

In ancient Greek discourse on happiness, rarely does one find a precise lexical definition of any of the terms we have encountered so far. More common is to find a description of happiness or the means to achieving happiness, and the authors do not tend to differentiate between the two options. It is vital, then, to consider some additional passages that give more precise formulations of the relationship between virtue, externals (i.e., external goods), and happiness, for the means of achieving happiness were as important to these ancient authors as the end.

We might divide views on happiness into those that see either virtue or pleasure as a necessary means. Commoners conceived of happiness as consisting of wealth, health, and other aspects of prosperity, but possessing these goods does not amount to happiness. Rather, they provide the means by which one may experience pleasure, which purportedly would generate happiness. For example, health is the opposite of sickness, which is painful, so health causes pleasure (the avoidance of pain). Wealth permits the purchase of necessary and luxury goods, whose consumption causes pleasure. Honor causes a pleasurable sense of satisfaction, and so on.

Commoners and even some philosophers held to a hedonistic route to happiness through the pleasure that arises from abundant externals. According to Aristotle, the masses believed that increasing property would increase pleasure, which would result in the good life (*Pol.* 1258a). According to Plato, "pleasures and pains and desires are a part of human nature, and on them every mortal being must of necessity hang and depend with the most eager interest" (*Leg.* 732e). A statesman must convince the people that a law would cause pleasure before they would support it, even if pleasure was not the actual rationale for the law. In Aristophanes's *The Birds*, Peisetaerus enumerates the "good things" that "men love exceedingly" as locusts not devouring their vine blooms, insects not devouring their fig trees, etc. (*Av.* 587–588). While these "good things" are not lavish or excessive, they do portray what the masses thought would bring them happiness. Virtue is nowhere to be found on the list. Aristophanes also devoted an entire play to Plutus, the god "wealth," in which the poor but virtuous people hatch a plan to depose Zeus and enthrone and worship Plutus as the highest god, who in return would reward the virtuous with great wealth. Whatever the playwright thinks of this view of wealth, he at least implies that the people long for it greatly.

A sustained argument in favor of the hedonistic thesis is made by Callicles, who debates the matter with Socrates in Plato's *Gorgias*. Callicles argues that the temperate and self-controlled are slaves to themselves, and no slaves are happy (491e).[12] Those with resources and power to enjoy them ought to satisfy their desires for maximal happiness. Most cannot fulfill their desires, so they condemn hedonism and licentiousness to disguise their own

---

12 Aristippus went one step further, not equating pleasure and happiness, but making happiness (εὐδαιμονία) the means to pleasure, which is man's end (Diog. Laert. 2.88).

impotence. He concludes, "luxury and licentiousness and liberty, if they have the support of force, are virtue and happiness" (ἀρετή τε καὶ εὐδαιμονία; 492c).[13] Plato apparently believes that Callicles represents the view of most people: "you are now stating in clear terms what the rest of the world thinks indeed, but are loth to say" (492d). Both Callicles and Plato believe that most commoners are hedonists, but the two give divergent explanations for why they veil their hedonism: to disguise their impotence (Callicles) or to avoid being judged (Plato).

To counter Callicles's claim, Socrates employs a *reductio ad absurdum* by considering a man who is constantly itchy and continually scratching. Such a person who has continual displeasure that requires continual relief is, according to Callicles, among the happiest of citizens. Callicles is unwilling to admit any problematic implications of his view, but Socrates seems certain that he has succeeded in his *reductio* (and continues with other examples of the same kind). The conclusion is that pleasure cannot be identified as a sufficient cause of happiness or identified as happiness itself.

A more nuanced version of the hedonistic thesis comes from the Epicureans, who held that "pleasure is the beginning and end of the blessed life (τὴν ἡδονὴν ἀρχὴν καὶ τέλος λέγομεν εἶναι τοῦ μακαρίως ζῆν), for this is our first and kindred good" (Diog. Laert. 10.129). But "pleasure" is not defined as indulgence; rather, it means "not feeling any pain or any mental turmoil" (10.131–132). Every pleasure is "a good thing," and every pain "a bad thing," but not every pleasure is worth choosing because it may create a net displeasure. Likewise, some pains are worth choosing because they will create a net pleasure (10.130). Because of this need for discernment, he concludes that "the greatest good is wisdom" and that "there is no way to live pleasantly without living wisely." So, Epicurus seems to define happiness as pleasure, understood as the avoidance of pain, and he concludes that the virtue of wisdom is required for achieving maximal pleasure.

Turning from pleasure to virtue, we find that most of the Greek philosophers understood virtue to be necessary for happiness,

---

13 Translation in LCL 166: 413.

but they differed in their understanding of virtue and of the role that externals played in conjunction with virtue. Christopher Vlastos has suggested three ways that virtue and happiness can be related.[14] First, virtue can be an instrumental means of happiness and not valued for its own sake. Second, virtue is not only desirable for its own sake but also because it is the principal part of happiness, although other elements may contribute to happiness. Third, virtue itself is happiness, and nothing else may contribute to happiness.

Socrates's position is that virtue (and the pursuit of further virtue) is happiness, while externals are immaterial. He says his accusers cannot harm him (i.e., damage his happiness) because he is a better man than they (Plato, *Ap.* 30c–d). No evil can happen to a good man in life or death (*Ap.* 41d). All good things come through virtue (*Ap.* 30b). One's standing in education and justice (i.e., virtue) is *all* that determines happiness (Plato, *Gorg.* 470e).[15] In *Euthydemus* 279–283, he argues that externals cannot be used rightly and may even be used detrimentally without wisdom and knowledge to guide the person. He concludes that externals are indifferent, wisdom the only good, and ignorance the only evil. As R. Kraut summarizes, Socrates held that "human well-being does not consist in wealth, power, or fame, but in virtue; that so long as one remains a good person one is immune to misfortune."[16]

---

14 Christopher Vlastos, "Happiness and Virtue in Socrates' Moral Theory," *Topoi* 4 (1985): 4.

15 Vlastos has argued that these should be read as hyperbolic comparatives, as when we tell someone that doing a favor is "no problem at all" ("Happiness and Virtue," 3–22). He adduces evidence, mainly from *Gorgias*, that Socrates viewed externals as "mini-constituents" of happiness. But *Gorgias* probably reflects Plato's emerging ideas, since it falls within the later portion of his "early dialogues." E.g., Richard Kraut says *Gorgias* "is one of the latest in this group—and probably *the* latest—for it contains a number of features that link it with dialogues that do not belong to this early period." Richard Kraut, "Introduction to the Study of Plato," in *The Cambridge Companion to Plato*, ed. Richard Kraut (Cambridge University Press, 1993), 4. For a list of the differences between *Gorgias* and the earlier Socratic dialogues, see Plato, *Gorgias*, trans. Terence Irwin (Clarendon Press, 1979), 1–12. So even if *Gorgias* does portray externals as "mini-constituents" of happiness, this view likely stems from Plato, not Socrates.

16 Kraut, "Introduction to the Study of Plato," 4.

Plato concurred with Socrates that virtue was preeminent for happiness, but he did admit a role for externals, albeit minuscule. His argument in *Philebus* is that, while dialectic and a perception of the Forms is the greatest good, one would not want wisdom or dialectic without any pleasure whatsoever, and so "we should seek the good, not in the unmixed life but in the mixed" (*Phileb.* 60e–61b). Indeed, if *Gorgias* portrays Plato's ideas, then he categorizes "wisdom and health and wealth" as "goods," which implies that they contribute somehow to happiness (*Gorg.* 467e–468b). The key to maximal happiness is in the proper priorities: "mind is ten thousand times nearer and more akin to the nature of the conqueror than pleasure" (*Phileb.* 67a).

Epicurus's position was similar to Plato's, but he admitted the need for at least simple and necessary goods. These goods are needed because they generate pleasure, which generates happiness. One should not rely heavily on lavish externals for happiness but should instead be content with meager and plain goods (Diog. Laert. 10.131–132). In the long run, this simplicity will bring more happiness because, first, simple broth can bring the same amount of pleasure as lavish meals if the hunger is great enough. Second, health will fare better with simple, healthy foods. Third, we will be better able to handle the downturns of fate when prosperity eludes us. Epicurus lived out what he taught, living simply and frugally, according to Diogenes Laertius (10.11).

Aristotle took an even firmer stance on externals: they are required for flourishing. Flourishing is difficult, if not impossible, without friends, some wealth, and some political power (*Eth. nic.* 1099b). Of these, friends are the most important (*Eth. nic.* 1169b). The difference between the extreme positions of Socrates and Aristotle is their conception of happiness. Socrates's conception has only to do with being wise or virtuous and pursuing to grow in it, which will make one happy. Aristotle, on the other hand, views happiness as an active concept (hence the translation "flourishing") such that one's exercise of virtue *is* happiness. Since man is a "social animal," the intellectual virtues are not enough to fulfill our end. Relational virtues such as magnanimity are also required, and such activity requires a sufficient amount of resources and friendships.

The philosophers discussed so far at least agreed that one can grow in virtue and thus grow in happiness. The Stoics disagreed, claiming that virtue and vice do not vary by degree. Virtue is knowledge. Thus, one may either have a stable character that knows the virtues and acts in accordance with them or not. Diogenes Laertius and others give analogies to support this point: a stick is either straight or crooked; a man drowns whether he is one or hundreds of feet from the surface; however close one is to his destination, he has not yet arrived.[17] Someone is either wise and virtuous or not, and only the former will be happy—and necessarily so.[18] Such a dichotomy eliminated any progress *in* virtue, but the Stoics did speak of progress *toward* virtue. "Now if it is virtue that holds out the promise thus to create happiness and calm and serenity, then assuredly progress toward virtue is progress toward each of these states of mind" (Epictetus, *Diatr.* 1.4). To understand this view better, K. Ierodiakonou suggests the analogy of the body's steady decline toward death. One can advance toward death and be closer to it than others while being alive at all times until that point. Similarly, one can advance from vice *toward* virtue, being all the time vicious but ever-nearing virtue until finally achieving it in a singular moment of fruition. At that point, one would become happy.

While the Stoics disagreed with Socrates's idea of advancing in virtue, they agreed with him that externals are unnecessary for happiness. Epictetus advised not to attach oneself to externals because they can be stripped away. To let externals dictate one's happiness would make one a slave (Epictetus, *Diatr.* 2.2; 3.24; 4.4). More fully:

> If he thinks that his good and his interest be in these things only which are free from hindrance and in his own power,

---

17 See a clear formulation in Diog. Laert. 7.127 and a fuller discussion in Katerina Ierodiakonou, "How Feasible Is the Stoic Conception of *Eudaimonia*?," in *The Quest for the Good Life: Ancient Philosophers on Happiness*, ed. Øyvind Rabbås, Eyjólfur K. Emilsson, Hallvard Fossheim, and Miira Tuominen (Oxford University Press, 2015), 184–187, and the ancient sources curated therein.

18 Whether virtue can be lost or not was a matter of debate between Chryssipus (yes) and Cleanthes (no).

he will be free, prosperous, happy .... But if he thinks that his good and his interest are in externals and in things which are not in the power of his will, he must of necessity be hindered, be impeded, be a slave to those who have the power over things which he admires and fears. (*Diatr.* 4.7)[19]

Perhaps one could view Epictetus's "detachment" discourse skeptically since he had formerly been a slave, but even the Stoic emperor Marcus Aurelius promoted detachment from externals. Neither intelligence, nor wealth, nor reputation, nor pleasure (all of which he had) would lead to happiness. Rather, happiness comes from living as nature wills according to virtue, that is, justice, temperance, manliness, and liberty (*Med.* 8.1). Summing up the Stoic view on externals, Diogenes Laertius (7.102) referred to them as "indifferent [ἀδιάφορα] in the category of preferred things." In the third century CE, Plotinus wrote a tractate named Περί Εὐδαιμονίας, in which he supports the Stoic position by arguing that happiness results from the proper use of intellect and not from anything external.

In sum, the ancient Greeks held a variety of views on the relationship between virtue, externals, and happiness. Many commoners and pure hedonists thought little of virtue and sought pleasure through externals. Pleasure was considered either happiness itself or the ultimate means to achieving happiness. Others, including most philosophers, believed virtue was necessary for happiness. Among these, externals fell on a spectrum ranging from detrimental (Stoics), to indifferent (Socrates and perhaps Plato), to minimally necessary (Epicureans), to vital (Aristotle). The difference arises from their differing conceptions of happiness. Ultimately, though, the two main contenders for bringing about happiness were (1) pleasure from externals and (2) virtue. The most thoughtful and civil thinkers held that virtue was indispensable. Among these thinkers, those who held happiness to be an active, social enterprise found externals to be essential, but even then, they had to

---

19 Translation in Epictetus, *The Discourses of Epictetus, with the Encheridion and Fragments*, trans. George Long (George Bell and Sons, 1890). See also *Diatr.* 4.4.

be used rightly according to moderation and wisdom. Those who held that happiness arises solely from possessing virtue or from the right use of the intellect had little use for externals in their theories of happiness.

Interpreting "Blessing" and "Happiness" in the New Testament

How could this conceptual background from the ancient Greeks help us interpret what Jesus and the apostles mean when they refer to the concept of happiness or blessing?

First, we could ask whether Jesus and the apostles were more like-minded with the thoughtful, virtue-oriented Greek thinkers or with the commoners who focused on externals and pleasures as what constitutes or creates the good life. It takes only a superficial survey of the Second Temple Jewish writings and the NT to discover that Jesus and the apostles (Jews themselves) would have found much more in common with the Greek philosophers when discussing virtue and the good life. For instance, many Jewish writings focused on the role of virtue (ἀρετή) in religion.[20] The term "virtue" is not abundant in the NT, but in Philippians 4:8 and 2 Peter 1:5 we do find the word used in ways that align with the usage by Greek philosophers and Jewish thinkers who adapted the terminology. We ought to suspect, then, that Jewish thinkers, including Jesus and the apostles, would have conceived of happiness or the good life in close relationship with virtue.

Second, we remember that even for the philosophers who thought virtue necessary for happiness, they varied on how they viewed external goods. From contextual considerations, then, it is theoretically possible that Jesus and the apostles could have considered externals as detrimental, indifferent, minimally necessary, or vital (or perhaps in some other way distinct to Jewish thought). Perhaps "vital" is the least likely hypothesis to bring to the NT.

---

20 Sib. Or. 3.234, cf. 2.139; Apoc. Sedr. 1.17; 3 Bar. 11.9, cf. 12.5; 14.2; T. Job 50.2; Apoc. Mos. 42.5; Wis 5:13; 8:7; Josephus, *Ant.* 1.6; Philo, *Worse* 60, 160; *Opif.* 8, 20, 73; Let. Aris. 1.122, 200, 215, 272, 277, 278; 4 Macc 1:2, 8, 10, 30; 2:10; 7:22; 9:8, 18, 31; 10:10; 11:2; 12:14; 13:24, 27; 17:12, 23.

Recall that Aristotle thought externals were vital because his conception of happiness was a social and an active concept ("flourishing"), that is, living in accord with man's end, which is "activity in conformity with virtue." Externals are needed to accommodate flourishing, which can only happen in a society. But Jesus and the apostles share different theological assumptions than Aristotle, so they are more likely to see man's end as something relating to God, not simply the activity of virtue. They are more likely to see virtue as a means, not an end. In 2 Peter 1:3–11, virtue is a *means* to increasing in the knowledge of Christ, confirming one's election, and ensuring that we enter the kingdom. In John 17:1, Jesus prays that through his character and actions at the cross, the Father would glorify the Son so the Son would glorify the Father. Perhaps the Westminster Catechism is not wrong in saying that man's chief end is to glorify God and enjoy him forever. Since virtue is not viewed as the chief end of man, we ought not to expect to find in the NT the idea that externals such as health and wealth are vital for happiness or blessedness. It is possible, though, that we could find more mitigated views on the necessity of external goods, such as the Epicurean attitude that they are minimally necessary.

At this point, we have enough of a cultural matrix through which to filter passages in the NT that talk about blessing, happiness, or the good life, and this was the objective of my essay. The next step would be to begin examining these passages in the NT to test our hypotheses about what they are likely to imply or state directly about virtue, externals, and happiness. To give only one brief example, consider Elizabeth's exclamation to Mary, "Blessed [εὐλογημένη] are you among women" (Luke 1:42). This young Jewish girl had just discovered that she would give birth to a miraculous son. She would be considered a fornicator by her family and society. Her betrothed (Joseph) initially resolved to annul the betrothal. This announcement to her came with no promise of externals, whether increased health, wealth, honor, or anything else. And yet Elizabeth calls "blessed" whom the Greeks would have called δυστυχής ("unfortunate"). She is "blessed" not because of any externals, but because of the supernatural favor bestowed upon her and her virtuous response to and attitude toward the angelic news. From this one example, we might form an initial hypothesis that the NT portrays externals as either indifferent or potentially detrimental. Other passages could suggest otherwise, but such a study is beyond the scope of this essay.

Conclusion

I have attempted to quickly survey ancient Greek conceptions of the concept of the good life, focusing on passages that explicitly refer to the concept through the variety of lexemes available in Classical and Koine Greek. I have then suggested that Jesus and the apostles would have thought similarly to the Greek philosophers who argued that virtue is necessary for the good life and, to a greater or lesser extent, saw a diminished role for externals. Finally, I have provided some thoughts on how this study could be extended into studying passages in the NT that refer to the concept of the good life, and how the cultural matrix I have provided would help us to form initial hypotheses that are more likely than not. Of course, I have only surveyed ancient Greek thought on the good life. Jesus and the apostles also communicated with those who were influenced by Roman religion, Jewish religion, a variety of political situations and socio-economic statuses, local church leaders, and more. Further research could provide views on the good life from these different domains, which would create an even more nuanced cultural matrix.

The purpose of this study was to consider whether prosperity theology (that blessing amounts to or is affected by abundant externals) was a plausible hypothesis to bring to the NT writings, given the construction of a cultural matrix. It seems clear from this investigation that the answer is no. There is no *a priori* reason to believe that first-century Jewish spiritual leaders writing to Greek-speaking audiences would refer to the concept of the good life solely or predominantly in terms of pleasure or externals. That is not to say that it would be impossible to prove from the NT writings themselves that Jesus and the apostles viewed blessing and happiness as consisting in externals such as health and wealth. My conclusion is simply that such a view would have a long, arduous, uphill climb, because not only would this mean that the ethics of Jesus and the apostles had more in common with that of typical Greek pagans and licentious hedonists, but it would also mean that they would risk miscommunication when writing to religious communities in which we know virtue, rather than externals, was stressed so highly.

9

"To Prosper" or צלח in Genesis 39

Philip Suciadi Chia

Introduction

THE HEBREW WORD צלח appears seven times in the book of Genesis (24:21, 40, 42, 56; 39:2, 3, 23). In Genesis 39, צלח occurs in a *hiphil* participle form. This research will attempt to argue that human righteousness and God's promise do not eliminate suffering, and suffering does not eliminate prosperity. Therefore, this paper will appeal to key words in the narrative, the narration context, and the parallelism of the passage to achieve its goal. It will also look at the *Testament of Joseph* to further corroborate its thesis.

Key Words

This article uses Waltke's key words to argue that human righteousness and God's promise do not eliminate suffering, and suffering does not eliminate prosperity. Although Waltke mentions that "Lord," "everything," "house," "in his hands," and "eyes" are the key words of Genesis 39:1–41:57,[1] this article focuses on "Lord," "everything," and "in his hands."

Despite his covenant with the patriarch, God remains hidden in the background of the narrative, allowing Joseph to experience

---

[1] They serve to link the scenes and build the tension between exaltation and humiliation. Bruce K. Waltke, *Genesis: A Commentary* (Zondervan, 2001), 517. Throughout this chapter, all Bible translations are my own.

much suffering.[2] The name "Lord" appears eight times in chapter 39 (39:2, 3 [2x], 5 [2x], 21, 23 [2x]). These appearances signal the important role of God's sovereignty in directing Joseph's life.[3] The *hophal* stem of ירד, for instance, denotes Joseph's going down to Egypt as the work of the Lord.[4] In spite of Joseph being rejected and sold by his brothers and abandoned in Egypt, the Lord is with him. Longacre argues that the name of the Lord appears at the darkest moment of Joseph's life.[5] Despite the appearance of the name of YHWH, God rarely appears in the Joseph story, and never to Joseph.[6] Also, Joseph neither sees God nor hears him speak. God is more a hidden influence rather than a character on stage *in spite of the righteousness of Joseph in Genesis 39*.[7] As Sarna notes, "There are no direct divine revelations or communications to Joseph. He builds no altars. He has no associations with cultic centers. God never openly and directly intervenes in his life."[8] Therefore, despite the faithfulness of Joseph and God's promise to the patriarch, Joseph still experiences suffering.

Suffering also does not eliminate prosperity. This thesis is supported by the words "everything" and "in his hands." These words are mentioned five times in Genesis 39 (39:3, 4, 5 [2x], 6). They emphasize God's unrestrained presence with Joseph and the extent of Joseph's exaltation. Waltke believes that the phrase "in his hands" signals Joseph's success (39:3, 4, 6, 8).[9] Cotter also states that Joseph's success is tied to his hands six times (39:3, 4, 6, 8, 22, 23).[10] Rabbi Yaakov Culi says that blessings usually require a base

---

2 Robert E. Longacre, *Joseph: A Story of Divine Providence: A Text Theoretical and Textlinguistic Analysis of Genesis 37 and 39–48* (Eisenbrauns, 1989), 43.

3 Waltke, *Genesis*, 518.

4 Elie Munk, *The Call of The Torah*, vol. 2, *An Anthology of Interpretation and Commentary on the Five Books of Moses, Genesis*, pt. 2 (Feldheim, 1980), 844.

5 Longacre, *Joseph*, 43.

6 Susan Niditch, *Underdogs and Tricksters: A Prelude to Biblical Folklore* (Harper & Row, 1987) 105.

7 D. Patrick, *The Rendering of God in the Old Testament*, OBT (Fortress, 1981), 22.

8 Nahum M. Sarna, *Genesis: Be-reshit: The Traditional Hebrew Text with New JPS Translation* (Jewish Publication Society, 1989), 254.

9 Waltke, *Genesis*, 518.

10 David W. Cotter, *Genesis*, Berit Olam (Liturgical Press, 2003), 289.

and cannot operate in a vacuum. Elisha, for example, had to begin with a pot of oil to fill up many barrels for his widow neighbor (1 Kgs 4:2). Without this pot, the miracle could not have happened. Joseph, on the other hand, does not follow this pattern. He had absolutely nothing, but he experienced a blessing. Genesis literally says that the dungeon warden "did not see anything in his hand, yet whatever he did, God made him succeed." The jailer kept Jospeh in prison, not because he wanted his work, but because he was fond of him.[11] These two key words reveal Joseph's prosperity in the midst of his unwanted situation and location.

Narration Context[12]

Human Righteousness Does Not Eliminate Suffering

Is Joseph a righteous man? Rabbi Yaakov Culi in the *Torah*

---

11 Rabbi Yaakov Culi, Isaac ben Moses Magriso, Aryeh Kaplan, Zvi Faier, Shmuel Yerushalmi, and Eliyahu Touger, *Torah Anthology Book Three: MeAm lo'ez* (Maznaim, 1977-1987), 318-319.

12 The final form of Genesis 39-41 moves from Joseph being a mere slave (39:1) to becoming the second leader in Egypt, the one to whom all the world is coming to preserve their lives (41:57). Clearly, therefore, this section has a neat narrative closure, and the broad sweep of these chapters outlines the rise of Joseph. It is important to view this account of the rise of Joseph as a cohesive section, for the tension introduced by Joseph's enslavement is not resolved until chap. 41. By way of contrast, if the analysis were to be of chap. 39 alone, then a commonly observed feature is that the chapter begins and ends with the reminder that God was with Joseph (vv. 2-3, 21-23). This motif, it has been suggested, brackets the remaining material and gives the theme for the chapter. Claus Westermann, *Genesis 37-50* (Augsburg, 1986), 60-61; John Skinner, *A Critical and Exegetical Commentary on Genesis*, ICC (T&T Clark, 1930), 457-460; Walter Brueggemann, *Genesis*, IBC (John Knox Press, 1982), 319-320; Terence E. Fretheim, "The Book of Genesis," in *The New Interpreter's Bible: General Articles & Introduction, Commentary, & Reflections for Each Book of the Bible, Including the Apocryphal/Deuterocanonical Books* (Abingdon Press, 1994), 609; John S. Kselman, "The Book of Genesis: A Decade of Scholarly Research" *Int* 45, no. 4 (1991): 380-392. Genesis 39 begins with the promising start of God being with Joseph (who prospers and has his hopes raised), and concludes with his hopes being unfairly dashed (imprisoned; forgotten by the cupbearer). "The Lord was with Joseph" also serves as the inclusion of chap. 39. Wilson argues that 39:2-6 speaks about the same thing as 39:21-23: the divine blessing of Joseph. Both passages, according to Wilson,

Anthology suggests that God was with Joseph because he constantly used God's name. Rabbi Yaakov Culi further continues that Joseph prayed to the Lord three times a day, as did all his family. As he retells the story, Potiphar noticed Joseph praying secretly and asked, "If you would, tell me what you are whispering about. Maybe you are trying to conjure up a magic spell. If you are, let me tell you something. We know that ten measures of sorcery were given to the world, and of them, nine were taken by Egypt!" Joseph, then, replied, "Nothing of the sort. I am merely praying that God grants me favor in your eyes." Potiphar asked more, "If you are praying, where is your god? I do not see any of your gods here. I would like to see your god." Joseph answered, "That is impossible. My God is invisible. To see him is beyond the power of any being."[13] Although the interpretation of Rabbi Yaakov Culi is fascinating, the book of Genesis does not provide such information. In other words, the Bible does not inform the readers about Joseph's daily righteousness before the Lord. However, the book's silence does not mean that Joseph was not a righteous man. Through the story of Joseph and Potiphar's wife juxtaposes Joseph's righteousness with Judah's wickedness (Gen 39:7–19; cf. Gen 38). However, in spite of Joseph's righteousness, he still experiences slander and mistreatment which lead him to the prison (39:20). This story makes clear that human righteousness does not eliminate suffering.

God's Promise Does Not Eliminate Suffering

Genesis 39:1 mentions that Joseph was bought by Potiphar from the Ishmaelites, although Genesis 37:36 states that Joseph was sold by the Midianites.[14] Rabbi Yaakov Culi in the *Torah Anthology*

---

recount the steady rise of Joseph against the backdrop of adversity. Again, Yahweh is mentioned (vv. 21, 23 as in vv. 2, 3, 5, yet not in 39:7–19 or 40:1–22), but without being foregrounded and without any face-to-face encounter between Joseph and his God. Lindsay Wilson, *Joseph Wise and Otherwise: The Intersection of Wisdom and Covenant in Genesis 37–50* (Paternoster, 2004), 96, 110.

13 Culi et al., *Torah Anthology Book Three*, 300–301.

14 Verse 1 serves as a hinge of chaps. 37 and 39 together by recapitulating the situation at the end of chap. 37 (37:36). This verse returns the reader's focus to Joseph and smooths the narrative transition between these two chapters.

argues that this purchasing denotes Potiphar is a smart trader. White men usually sell black men as slaves. However, Joseph was sold by black men. It indicates that Joseph was kidnapped, and his relatives might come and want him back. Therefore, before Potiphar bought Joseph, the Midianites must bring someone to vouch for them. In this case, the Ishmaelites were brought into the narrative to validate that Joseph had been bought from them, and with this, the deal was finalized.[15] Another interpretation is that Joseph was initially purchased by the Ishmaelites. However, the Midianites bought Joseph along the way. Then, the Midianites were not able to go too far because the other Ishmaelites attacked them and stole Joseph. Then, the other Ishmaelites brought Joseph to Egypt and sold to Potiphar. When the Midianites came to Egypt, they were able to regain Joseph by bringing their grievance to the court. Potiphar, then, repurchased Joseph from the Midianites.[16] Ramban, however, maintains that the Ishmaelites caravan owners hauled Joseph to Egypt on behalf of the Midianites. Therefore, the sale was attributed indirectly to them since they were the ones who had brought him down there, and Torah refers to them alternately as Ishmaelites and Midianites.[17] Similarly, Ibn Ezra thinks that Torah refers to the Ishmaelites and the Midianites interchangeably because they are kinsmen.[18] Gur Aryeh explains that the term "Ishmaelites" was the common designation for the clan which included the Midianites.[19] In spite of the debates of the identity of the Ishmaelites and the Midianites, this story reveals that the entire narrative was directed by the Lord. Why? The Ishmaelites were the descendants of Hagar, the slave of Abraham and Sarah. Potiphar,

---

Gordon J. Wenham, *Genesis 16–50*, WBC 2 (Word Books, 1994), 373; W. Lee Humphreys, *Joseph and His Family: A Literary Study* (University of South Carolina Press, 1988), 58; George W. Coats, *Genesis with an Introduction to Narrative Literature*, FOTL 1 (Eerdmans, 1983), 276.

15 Culi et al., *Torah Anthology Book Three*, 299.
16 Culi et al., *Torah Anthology Book Three*, 300.
17 Meir Zlotowitz and Nosson Scherman, *Bereishis Genesis: A New Translation with a Commentary Anthologized from Talmudic, Midrashic and Rabbinic Sources* (Mesorah, 1977), 1701.
18 Zlotowitz and Scherman, *Bereishis*, 1701.
19 Zlotowitz and Scherman, *Bereishis*, 1701.

nevertheless, was a descendant of Ham, whom Noah cursed to be a slave to his brothers (9:25). Joseph, on the other hand, is the firstborn of Rachel, Jacob's favorite wife. Joseph, however, becomes a slave. The process of becoming a slave involves both the Ishmaelites and Potiphar. It is ironic, but this irony is a clear sign of God's orchestration.[20] Although Joseph has gone down to Egypt and gone down in status (once a favorite son, now he is a slave), and Jacob, his father, is no longer with him, the Lord is still with Joseph (39:2, 3, 5, 21, 23).[21] It seems that the narrator links God's presence with Joseph to his presence with the patriarch.[22] The Lord uses Joseph's suffering to fulfill his promise to preserve his people (50:20). In other words, God's promise does not eliminate suffering, but the Lord can use suffering to keep his promise to Abraham, Isaac, and Jacob.

Suffering Does Not Eliminate Prosperity

Genesis 39:2 begins with "the Lord was with Joseph." The expression "the Lord was with Joseph" indicates success, prosperity, or victory. The word "success" is also used when describing Abraham's servant in Gen 24:21, etc.[23] In the story of Joseph, this sentence communicates God's beneficent presence is experienced even in times of suffering (26:3, 24, 28; 28:15, 20; 31:3).[24] While Joseph's future is uncertain (alone in foreign land, separated from his family), the narrator deliberately mentions "the Lord" at the most difficult moment in Joseph's life to communicate that Joseph is not alone. The Lord is with him.[25] God's presence brings success to Joseph's life (39:3, 23). Jewish sources record that this success includes the protection of Joseph from spiritual absorption by heathen circumstance and his enemies.[26] The theme of "the Lord was

---

20 Culi et al., *Torah Anthology Book Three*, 300.
21 Cotter, *Genesis*, 289.
22 Westermann, *Genesis 37–50*, 63.
23 Kenneth A. Mathews, *Genesis 11:27–50:26: An Exegetical and Theological Exposition of Holy Scripture*, NAC 1B (Holman Reference, 2005), 731.
24 Waltke, *Genesis*, 519.
25 Longacre, *Joseph*, 45; Westermann, *Genesis 37–50*, 62.
26 The connotation of God being "with" someone, an expression occurring often in the Scripture with the Hebrew word *'im* rather than *'ēṯ*, implies that the

with Joseph" forms the theological entrance to the Joseph story which finds its counterpart at the end with the concluding words of Joseph "God brought me here" (45:5–8; 50:17–21). Chapters 39–41 are the story of a rise, and this rise was made possible because the Lord was with Joseph.[27]

Genesis 39:3 describes that although he was in Potiphar's house, Joseph was under the Lord's blessing and guidance.[28] The Lord is with Joseph, and YHWH brings success to him. Jewish sources say that Potiphar sees unusual success in Joseph because he was supported by the Lord.[29] Rabbi Elie Munk says that Joseph's triumphant success in all that he did could only have been the result of a blessing from a supernatural source.[30] Joseph's success, nonetheless, was not usual given his adverse circumstances. Joseph was in the house of his master. The natural success usually comes to the master (or Potiphar), but in this case, it came to Joseph (or a slave).[31]

Genesis 39:23 serves an *inclusio*. Although Joseph reached the lowest point to which he was to sink, God's favor turned to him.[32] Just as in 39:3, the Lord's favor leads to Joseph's favor with his master, which the narrator describes in the same terms: "favor in the eyes" (39:4, 21).[33] The expression "in his hands" also communicates Joseph's success as well as God's providential role in that success (39:3, 22, 23). The threefold repetition of giving

---

Lord is watching over the details of man's various activities according to the degree of man's perfection (Ramban, "Moreh Nevuchim," in *Bereishis, Genesis: A New Translation with a Commentary Anthologized from Talmudic, Midrashic and Rabbinic Sources*. [New York: Mesorah Publications, 1977], 3:18). The word 'ēṯ also denotes an exegetical implication: not only was the Lord with Joseph, but with everyone with whom he came in contact. Compare the case of Lot who accumulated great wealth merely by virtue of accompanying Abraham. Zlotowitz and Scherman, *Bereishis*, 1701.

27 Westermann, *Genesis 37–50*, 62; Wilson, *Joseph Wise and Otherwise*, 99.
28 Victor P. Hamilton, *The Book of Genesis. Chapters 18–50*, NICOT (Eerdmans, 1995), 460.
29 Zlotowitz and Scherman, *Bereishis*, 1702.
30 Munk, *Genesis*, pt 2, 847.
31 Zlotowitz and Scherman, *Bereishis*, 1702; Wilson, *Joseph Wise and Otherwise*, 99.
32 Samson Raphael Hirsch, *Der Pentateuch* (J. Kauffmann, 1920), 565.
33 Wilson, *Joseph Wise and Otherwise*, 111.

confirms God's blessing in the future (39:20, 21, 22).[34] As Wenham says, that this statement implies quite real protection and promotion in the matters of Joseph's external life, not protection from distress, but rather in the midst of distress.[35] Ambrose asks, "Where does God's mercy not enter?"[36] In the story of Joseph, he sees that Joseph found favor of this sort; he who had been shut up in the prison kept the locks of the prison, while the jailer withdrew from his post and entrusted all the prisoners to his power.[37] Just as Caesarius of Arles says that the Lord never deserts Joseph, but he visits his own even in prison.[38]

The narration context of Genesis 39:2, 3, and 23 communicates that Joseph's suffering does not eliminate God's blessing or prevent him from prospering. Joseph is still in the difficult places, both Potiphar's house and prison, yet he succeeds.

Parallelism

The first parallelism focuses on Joseph's prosperity. God is making Joseph a successful man in spite of his situations and locations. Despite the malicious intentions of his brothers in Genesis 37, Genesis 39:3 provides the reasons why Potiphar highly regarded Joseph and placed him in charge of his affairs (v. 4): the Lord gave him

---

34 Waltke, *Genesis*, 523.

35 Wenham, *Genesis 16–50*, 381.

36 Ambrose, *De Joseph* cited in Mark Sheridan and Thomas C. Oden, *Genesis 12–50*, ACCSOT 2 (InterVarsity, 2002), 258.

37 Ambrose, *De Joseph* cited in Sheridan and Oden, *Genesis 12–50*, 258.

38 Caesarius of Arles, *Sermones* cited in Sheridan and Oden, *Genesis 12–50*, 258. Yahuda mentions that this prison is a well-known fortress of great strategic and military importance. From the edict of Haremheb, Joseph's prison is a place of internment for criminals. However, Genesis 39:20, 22, and 40:3 communicate that this is not an ordinary prison, but a special jail for dangerous criminals and political offenders. Otherwise, the narrator would not have expressly mentioned that it was a place in which the king's prisoners were incarcerated, an explanation which indicates the concern of the narrator to emphasize that it was in a prison for dangerous criminals and traitors that Pharaoh's butler and baker were interned. The character of this penal establishment is best illustrated by its description in Genesis 40:3 as a specific place of confinement under the supervision of the chief executioner. Abraham Shal Yahuda, *The Language of the Pentateuch in Its Relation to Egyptian* (Oxford University Press, 1933), 40.

success in everything he did. This measure of success corresponds to the comprehensive assignment that Potiphar gives him to oversee "everything he owned" (v. 4). This encompassing assignment for a slave was staggering, meriting mentions of it in the chapter (vv. 4, 5 [2x], 8). Precisely what he achieved and how it came to his master's attention is unstated, although "blessing" in Genesis typically involves material wealth (24:35; 26:12; 30:27, 30). The narrative indicates that the source of his achievement was a divine grant, not a man's intellect or ability.[39] The same language describing his ascent in Potiphar's house (vv. 1–6) is also used in verses 21–23 to explain Joseph's favored status in prison, despite the manipulations of a scorned seductress.[40] As Mathews comments,

> The human figures in the large biblical landscape act as free agents out of the impulses of a memorable and often fiercely assertive individuality, but the actions they perform all ultimately fall into the symmetries and recurrences of God's comprehensive design. At the lowest point in his life, in the bonds of a foreign place, with no friend and no prospect of release, God initiated the step that brought about deliverance for Joseph, his kin, and the world (cf. Ps. 105:17–22). In both the wilderness pit and in Potiphar's prison, the Lord's presence ("the Lord was with him") delivered the young Hebrew from death.[41]

Therefore, this parallelism demonstrates human righteousness does not eliminate suffering, and suffering does not eliminate prosperity.

The second parallelism focuses on "kindness" in the story of Potiphar and the jailer. Both of them are identified as the chief of the guard (v. 1) and of the jail (v. 21). The text also elaborates on the earlier impression. "He [i.e., the jailer] showed him kindness" recalls the former narrative and also anticipates the prison scene. Verses 21–23 are not, however, a pure repetition of verses 3–4. In the former narrative, Potiphar extends "kindness" (v. 4).

---

39 Mathews, *Genesis 11:27–50:26*, 732.
40 Mathews, *Genesis 11:27–50:26*, 738.
41 Mathews, *Genesis 11:27–50:26*, 738.

This narrative, on the other hand, reports that the Lord was the one who showed "kindness" to Joseph (v. 21). This coupling of human involvement and divine intercession reflects the author's theology, for it was ultimately the Lord who propelled Potiphar to bestow special privileges on Joseph. The word "kindness" appears again in Joseph's plea to the king's cupbearer, whose dream Joseph had favorably interpreted (40:14).[42] Once again, this parallelism emphasizes that suffering does not eliminate prosperity or receiving kindness.

The third parallelism focuses on "authority." Verses 22–23 emphasize, as in the earlier case (vv. 6, 9), that nothing was withheld from Joseph's oversight in the prison. "All" prisoners and "all" activities fell under Joseph's supervision (v. 22 and vv. 5–6). The warden's motivation for endowing Joseph with exceptional authority ("the Lord gave him success," v. 23) was the same as that of Potiphar (vv. 2–3) and ultimately of Pharaoh (41:38–41).[43] In summary, although Joseph is in a foreign land as a slave and in prison as a prisoner, he still receives an authority to supervise all. Suffering does not eliminate prosperity.

Word Studies

Lexical Analysis

The Hebrew word צלח only occurs in the *qal* and *hiphil* stems. The basic meaning of צלח in the *qal* is to prosper. Although there is a causative nuance in the *hiphil* stem ("to cause to prosper"), the meaning "to prosper" remains.[44] BDB and *HALOT* translate צלח as prosperous in Genesis 39:2. However, both lexica understand צלח in a causative meaning or "to cause to prosper" in Genesis 39:3 and 39:23 because it is preceded by a direct object.[45] צלח is related to סָלַח, perhaps also שָׁלַח.[46] סָלַח can refer to remitting

---

42 Mathews, *Genesis 11:27–50:26*, 738.
43 Mathews, *Genesis 11:27–50:26*, 738.
44 BDB, 852; *HALOT*, vol. 3: 1072.
45 The object is כֹּל אֲשֶׁר in Gen 39:3, while Gen 39:23 simply uses a relative particle אֲשֶׁר.
46 Hirsch, *Der Pentateuch*, 559.

an unforgiven sin that obstructs the path of a man's life. סְלִיחָה means "to allow a procedure to be unhindered." שָׁלַח is to send or to move something towards a goal. צלח communicates a progress towards the goal and overcoming obstacles. Applying this definition to Genesis 39, צלח communicates that Joseph was a man who brought everything he undertook to a happy conclusion. Even though he was young, poor, a foreigner, and of the lowest class, Joseph succeeded in everything just because it was he who did it. This success demonstrated the power of the Lord.[47]

The Usage of the Participle

The use of the participle מַצְלִיחַ in 39:2–3, 23 suggests that the prosperity of Joseph becomes a pattern in his life.[48] Chrysostom understands this word as "a man of means."[49] It means that everything went well for Joseph; grace from on high preceded him everywhere, and the grace that flourished with regard to Joseph was so obvious as to become plain even to his master, the chief steward. He was a young man, a stranger, a captive slave, yet his master entrusted him with his whole household.[50] Westermann understands מַצְלִיחַ as a man of achievement.[51] Ksav Sofer notes that this causative form denotes that Joseph's presence caused others to prosper as well.[52]

Cognate Languages

HALOT provides the list of cognate languages and their meanings related to צלח.[53]

---

47 Hirsch, *Der Pentateuch*, 560.
48 Hamilton, *Genesis: Chapters 18–50*, 460.
49 John Chrysostom, *Homiliae in Genesim* cited in Sheridan and Oden, *Genesis 12–50*, 248.
50 John Chrysostom, *Homiliae in Genesi*m cited in Sheridan and Oden, *Genesis 12–50*, 248.
51 Westermann, *Genesis 37–50*, 62.
52 Zlotowitz and Scherman, *Bereishis*, 1702.
53 *HALOT*, vol. 3: 1072.

- Biblical Aramaic: ṣlḥ means to make progress or to cause to do well
- Christian Palestinian Aramaic: ṣlḥ means to split or to thrive
- Jewish Aramaic: ṣlḥ means to be successful or to thrive.
- Egyptian Aramaic: mṣlḥ means either to split wood or to set wood on fire.
- Samaritan: ṣlḥ means to be successful.
- Arabic: ṣalaḥa means to thrive or to encourage.
- Tigré: ṣalḥa means to be well and ṣalḥāt to be successful.

Biblical Aramaic's translation "to make progress" denotes a progression. Joseph had lost control of his life when he was taken down to Egypt (39:1),[54] yet he was still progressing. In other words, progression could still occur in an unexpected situation. God might not change the situation, yet God could still progress Joseph.

The Arabic's and the Christian Palestinian Aramaic's translation, "to thrive," also communicate Joseph's development. In Genesis 37:3, the narrator reveals that Joseph is a golden boy since Jacob loves him more than all his sons. Genesis 39:1–2, however, highlights Joseph's new status: from a golden boy to a slave. In spite of his new status as a slave, God could still cause him to thrive.

The Jewish Aramaic, Samaritan, and Tigré translations clearly understand צלח as "success." Although Joseph is a foreigner, God could still make him succeed in a different location. Interestingly, as Takeuchi argues, although a righteous foreigner in the Bible acted amiably for the good in the right fear of God,[55] their safety is not guaranteed. In other words, Joseph's godliness does not warrant his security, yet God could still bless him in the midst of his insecurity. Egyptian Aramaic's translation, on the other hand, seems to communicate a figurative meaning in the light of Genesis 39.

---

54 As Waltke states, Gen 39:1 recapitulates 37:36, moving from "sold" to "bought"—after the parenthetical chap. 38—and so forms a transition from 37:36. Waltke, *Genesis*, 517.

55 Yu Takeuchi, "Outsiders Know Better? Introducing the 'Righteous Foreigners' in the Hebrew Bible and Their Significance," *CISMOR Conference on Jewish Studies* 9 (2017): 174–181.

In summary, cognate languages reveal that צלח means "to thrive, to be successful." Contextually, צלח does not change or eliminate Joseph's hard situation, new status, or place, yet Joseph could still progress or thrive.

Ancient Translations

In this section, the occurrences of the word צלח will be discussed in the light of ancient translations to see how these manuscripts understand the word צלח.

Hebrew Word צלח in Genesis 39:2		
Source	Text	Translation
Greek Septuagint	ἐπιτυγχάνων	To be successful
Hexapla (Ἀ)	κατευθυνόμενος	The one who prospers
Hexapla (Σ)	εὐοδούμενος	To be prosperous
ὁ συρ´	κατευοδούμενος	To be prosperous
Latin Vulgate	In cunctis prospere agens	In all (things), (the man is) going successfully
Samaritan	מצליח	To be prosperous
Aramaic Targum	מַצְלַח	To be prosperous
Syriac Peshitta	ܡܨܠܚ	To be successful
Syro-Hexapla (ܐ)	ܡܬܪܨܢܐ	The one who prospers
Syro-Hexapla (ܣ)	ܡܫܠܡ	To be firm or established

Hatch and Redpath reveal that ἐπιτυγχάνω is used to translate צלח in the *hiphil* stem.[56] LSJ records that ἐπιτυγχάνω as a participle means "to succeed in doing."[57] Literally, it means "man of success."[58] Therefore, regardless of Joseph's new situation, status and

---

56 HRCS, vol. 1:537.
57 LSJ, 669.
58 Hayim Tawil describes the development of צָלֵה as to proceed, pass, go (with speed) or to advance, progress, prosper, succeed. Hayim Tawil, "Hebrew צלח / הצלח, Akkadian *ešēru*/*šūšuru*: A Lexicographical Note," *JBL* 95, no. 3 (1976): 405–413.

place, he is still succeeding in what he is doing.

Aquila uses the rather unusual translation, κατευθυνόμενος, because its primary meaning is "to direct" or "to guide," although Sirach 29:18 also has "succeed in doing." It is also possible that Aquila wants to communicate the righteousness of Joseph (cf. Prov 15:8). In spite of Joseph's unfavored condition, he maintains a godly attitude, and he is still successful.

Hatch and Redpath point out that εὐοδόω is used to translate צלח in Ezra 5:8 by LXX.[59] While Symmachus has εὐοδόω, the meaning in passive voice is to have a prosperous journey.[60] Joseph has a prosperous journey in the midst of his rocky journey.[61]

The Latin Vulgate, interestingly, adds more information on the translation of צלח. The Vulgate does not only describe the success of Joseph, but also the area of his prosperity: all things.

The Syriac's translation is taken from צלח in the *qal* stem.[62] Literally, this word means "to bring prosperity" or "a good success." The Samaritan, Targum, and Peshitta also convey the connotation of prosperity. In other words, Joseph is prospering in the situation and place with a status that is out of his will.

Hebrew Word צלח in Genesis 39:3		
Source	Text	Translation
Greek Septuagint	εὐοδοῖ	To prosper
Latin Vulgate	gereret ... dirigi ...	To cause straight
Samaritan	מצליח	To be prosperous
Aramaic Targum	מַצְלַח	To be prosperous
Syriac Peshitta	ܡܨܠܚ	To be successful

The LXX uses a different word, εὐοδόω, for the very same word of צלח found in Genesis 39:2. The meaning is "to succeed" or "to prosper" in an active voice. Contextually, LXX communicates

---

59 HRCS, vol. 1:575.
60 LSJ, 724.
61 Philip Suciadi Chia, "A Critical Edition of the Hexaplaric Fragments of Genesis" (PhD diss., The Southern Baptist Theological Seminary, 2021), 579.
62 HRCS, 2:750.

the reason for Joseph's success is the Lord himself who prospers Joseph.

Vulgate interprets the word צלח as "to cause straight" or "to make success." In other words, the Lord goes (before Joseph) to arrange all things in Joseph's hands. Samartian, Targum, and Peshitta use the same translation "to be prosperous."

Hebrew Word צלח in Genesis 39:23		
Source	Text	Translation
Greek Septuagint	εὐώδου	To prosper
Latin Vulgate	*dirigebat*	To direct
Samaritan	מצליח	To be prosperous
Aramaic Targum	מַצְלַח	To be prosperous
Syriac Peshitta	ܡܨܠܚ	To be successful

The table above reveals that the translation of מַצְלִיחַ in this verse is similar to Genesis 39:3, particularly for the LXX's and Vulgate's translations. It is likely that the sentence "the Lord was with him" influenced both translations. The presence of God causes Joseph to prosper.

In summary, these word studies demonstrate that Joseph's righteousness does not merit God's blessing (39:23), and suffering in the house of Potiphar and in the prison do not eliminate prosperity (39:2, 3, 23).

Testament of Joseph

This article uses Stone's translation of the *Testament of Joseph*.[63] 1:5 describes Joseph's suffering when he was brought down to Egypt, but God never leaves him: "I was sold into slavery and the Lord of all freed me. I was led into captivity and his mighty hand aided me, I was beset by hunger and the same Lord himself nurtured me." 1:6

---

63 Michael E. Stone, *An Editio Minor of the Armenian Version of the* Testaments of the Twelve Patriarchs, Hebrew University Armenian Studies 11 (Peeters, 2012), 369–381.

describes God's presence in the prison: "I was alone and God comforted me, in sickness and the Most High was my visitor, in prison and the Most High made me graceful, in bonds and he loosed me." 1:7 describes God's deliverance in Potiphar's house: "amidst calumnies he defended me, in the bitter words of the Egyptians and he delivered me, amidst the envy of my fellow-slaves and he exalted me." God's presence resulted in Potiphar entrusting his house to Joseph (2:1). This story communicates that although Joseph suffers, God still delivers and prospers him.

The next verses show that, despite Joseph's righteousness in resisting sexual temptation, he still suffers. 2:2 describes Joseph's struggle against the shameless woman who urged him to sin with her, but the God of Israel delivered him from the burning fire. 3:3–4, 10 depicts Joseph's righteousness: "I would remember the words of the fathers of my father Jacob, and I would enter into (my) chamber, I would pray to the Lord. And I fasted for those seven years, and I appeared to the Egyptian as if I was living with luxury, for those who fast for God's sake receive grace of countenance. I was saying the words of the Most-High to her so that, perhaps, she would turn aside from her evil desire." Although Joseph was righteous, verse 2:3a pictures Joseph's suffering: "I was imprisoned, I was tortured, I was despised." Verses 2:3b–4, nevertheless, demonstrate God's blessing upon Joseph's hardship: "yet the Lord made me the object of the chief warder's compassion, because the Lord does not abandon those who fear him nor does he put them in darkness in bonds, nor in tribulations, nor in misfortunes."

8:5 continues speaking of Joseph's righteousness in the midst of his suffering: "while I was in detention, the Egyptian woman fell ill from sorrow, and she listened to me, how while I was in the dark house, I blessed the Lord continually with a glad voice and rejoicing I glorified God for he had set me apart, alone from the pretexts of the Egyptian woman." At the end, 9:5 and 11:6–7 summarize God's blessing upon Joseph in the foreign land: "while Joseph was in Potiphar's house, his wife bared her arms and breast and legs so that she herself might make Joseph stumble, and she adorned herself greatly, but the Lord preserved Joseph from her aggression. The Lord gave Joseph grace in the eyes of Potiphar, and he entrusted his house to Joseph. The Lord blessed Potiphar through Joseph and multiplied (his) silver and gold."

Conclusion

The story of Joseph, told both from biblical and non-biblical texts, reveals that suffering can happen to a righteous man who is a part of God's faithful covenant to Abraham. However, God is always with his people, and he can prosper them in the midst of their suffering like Joseph. Ephrem states that "Joseph was seventeen years old when he was sold. He was in the house of Potiphar for eleven years; [thus,] he was twenty-eight years old when his mistress revolted against him. He was delivered into the prison house for two years; [thus,] he was thirty years old when he stood before Pharaoh."[64] "But Joseph [rose] from the pit to the rule of the kingdom, and from disgrace to glorious honor."[65] The use of צלח ("to prosper") in Genesis 39 demonstrates that God's people often suffer, but God will bless his people through suffering.

---

64 Edwards G. Matthews Jr., *The Armenian Commentary on Genesis Attributed to Ephrem the Syrian*, CSCO 572–573 (Peeters, 1998), 137.

65 Matthews, *Armenian Commentary*, 143.

Index

Genesis

1	99	26:34–35	36
2:7	40	28:15	158
2:17	30, 39	28:20	158
3:14–19	30	30:27	161
3:15	32	30:30	161
3:17	30, 39-41, 82	31:3	158
3:17–18	82n12	37	30n7, 154n2, 159n27, 160
3:19	30, 39	37:3	164
3:22	30	37:36	156, 156n14, 164n54
3:23	30		
3:23–24	30	37–50	155n12, 156, 158n22,25, 159n27, 163n51
5	32		
9:25	158		
11	32	38	156
11:27–50:26	158n23, 161n39-41, 162n42-43	39	153-155, 153n1, 155n12, 157, 159, 161, 163-165, 167, 169
12:1–3	32, 34-35		
12–50	160n36-38, 163n49-50		
		39–41	155n12
13:2	75	39–48	154n2
13:2–6	77	39:1–2	164
13:5–6	75	39:2–3	163
16–50	157, 160n35	39:2–6	155n12
19:12–22	84n27	39:1	155n12, 156, 164
24:21	153, 158	39:1	167
24:22	75	39:2	153-154, 158, 160, 162, 165-166, 167
24:35	161		
24:40	153	39:3	153-154, 158-160, 162, 162n45, 166-167
24:42	153		
24:56	153		
26:3	158	39:4	154, 159
26:12	161	39:5	154, 158
26:24	158	39:6	154
26:28	158	39:7–19	156

39:8	154	Deuteronomy	
39:9	162	6	29, 37n15
39:4	160-161	6:2	37
39:6	162	6:4–7	29
39:10–14	90	6:6	37
39:20	156, 160	6:7	37
39:21	156n12, 158-162	6:8	37
39:21–23	155n12	8:17–18	42
39:22	154, 159-160, 162	12:7	70
39:23	153-154, 156n12, 158-159, 160, 162-163, 167	14:23–26	70
		15	36
		15:1–6	36
39:1–41:57	153	15:7–11	36
40:1–22	156	17	29, 37n15
40:3	160n38	17:14–20	29
40:14	162	17:17	38
41:38–41	162	29:29	43
41:57	155n12	31:6	133
45:5–8	159	31:8	133
47:20–23	75		
50:17–21	159	Joshua	
50:20	158	1:5	133
Exodus		Judges	
4:22–23	32	2:11	89n46
19:6	89	2:13	89n46
20:17	62, 71	2:19	89n46
23:14	70	3:6	89n46
24:15–16	92n59	3:7	89n46
28:17–21	90		
34:6–7	35	Ruth	
40:34–35	92n59	2:2–15	68
Leviticus		1 Samuel	
19:9–10	68	2:7	42
25	36		
25:1–7	36	2 Samuel	
25:4	36	7	32
25:20–22	36	7:14	36
26	31		
26:3–5	31	1 Kings	
26:6–8	32	4:2	155
26:9	32	6:20	90n50
26:11–13	31-32	8:10–12	92n59
26:12	88		

Ezra
    5:8   166
Job
    1:2–3   75
Psalms
    1:1   39
    1:3   33, 39
    1:6   34
    2   50, 91n54
    16:11   30
    19:7   38
    22:3   102n19
    32   38
    36:9   35
    49:1–2   61
    50:10   50
    105:17–22   161
    112:1–9   77
    118:6   133
    128   41

Proverbs
    1:1   29n6
    1:4   33
    1:7   34
    1:8   33
    1:8–19   30n7
    1:10–19   34
    1:18–19   34
    1:20–33   30n7
    1:29   34
    2:1–4   34
    2:5   34
    2:21–22   35
    2:20   35
    3   35-36, 36n14, 37n15
    3:1   37
    3:1–2   36-38
    3:1–8   40
    3:1–12   36, 38
    3:2   37
    3:3–4   36, 37
    3:5   38
    3:8   38
    3:9–10   38
    3:13   39
    3:14   39
    3:15   39
    3:16   39
    3:17   39
    3:18   35
    4:2–3   29
    6:1–19   30n7
    10:1   29n6
    10:11   35
    10:22   35
    13:7a   75
    13:14   35
    13:22   35, 77
    14:27   35
    15:8   166
    15:15–17   27
    16:22   35
    16:26   72
    23:20–21   69
    25:1   29n6
    28:7   69
    28:8   38n17, 77
    28:25   37n16
    30:8   77
    30:9   78

Ecclesiastes
    1:1   29
    1:2   39
    1:3   39
    1:8b   41
    1:16   29
    2:1–11   40
    2:3   40
    2:9   29
    2:11   40
    2:12–17   40
    2:14–16   40
    2:17   40
    2:18–26   40
    2:24–25   41

3:1–8	40	48:20–22	84n27
3:3	38	50:7	57
3:4	38	52:11–12	84n27
3:5–6	36	54:11–12	89, 93
3:6	38	55:1	82n17
3:7	38	60	86, 91, 93
3:9–10	36-37	60:1–2	92n59
3:9	40, 40n20	60:6	86
3:11	40-41	60:6b	91
3:11–12	36	60:7	86
3:12–13	41	60:9	86
3:14	41	60:11	87
3:16–17	43	60:13	87
3:19	40	60:17	86-87
3:20	40	60:19	92
3:22	41	60:19–20	92
4:1	42		
4:7–16	40	Jeremiah	
4:8	41	7	30n7
5:7	41	20	30n7
5:8	42	23:1–4	56
5:9	42	31:33	37
5:10	41	50:8–10	84n27
5:18	41	51:6–10	84n27
5:19	76	51:45–48	84n27
6:1–2	41, 76		
6:12	40	Ezekiel	
7:7	42	1	84
8:17	40	27:12–14	83
8:12–13	41	28:13	90
8:13	41	34	57
9:7–10	41	34:1–6	56
10:19	42	34:3	57
11:5–6	40	34:5	57
11:8–10	41	34:10	57
11:9	41		
12:7	40	Daniel	
12:8	39	3:12	89n46
12:10	39	3:14	89n46
12:11	39	3:17	89n46
12:13–14	41	3:18	89n46
		3:95	89n46
Isaiah		6:17	89n46
6:1–4	92n59	6:21	89n46
15	66n12	7	84

10	84	Mark	
Micah		7:20–23	71
2:2	71	8:31	53
		8:34	54
Zechariah		9:30–31	53
2:5	92	10:25	77
		10:33–34	53
Tobit		10:35–37	58
13:11	87, 92	10:38–40	58
13:11–16	93	10:41–45	59
13:16	86n35	10:45	59
		11:22	7, 12
Wisdom of Solomon		14:36	50, 58
5:13	149n20		
8:7	149n20	Luke	
		1:42	150
Sirach		2:37	89n47
29:18	166	2:52	38
		3:10	68
4 Maccabees		3:11	68
1:2	149n20	4:8	89n47
1:8	149n20	4:18	10n36
1:10	149n20	9:51	57
1:30	149n20	12:15	71
2:10	149n20	12:32	51
7:22	149n20	12:50	58
9:8	149n20	18:25	77
9:18	149n20	22:37	55
9:31	149n20		
10:10	149n20	John	
11:2	149n20	10:11	57
12:14	149n20	14:14	100
13:24	149n20	17:1	150
13:27	149n20	Acts	
17:12	149n20	10:23	130
17:23	149n20	21:16	130
		28:7	130
Matthew			
6:11	125n8	Romans	
6:19–21	76	1:25	89n47
11:19	70	3:30	51n9
13:22	77	5:12	39
19:24	77	6:1–2	49
28:18	50	6:6–7	49

7:7	62	4:8	149
8	52	4:11	63
8:1	49	4:12	42
8:9	51n9		
8:12–17	48	**Colossians**	
8:12	49	1:24	57
8:13	49		
8:14–15	49	**2 Thessalonians**	
8:16	50	1:6	51n9
8:17	50, 51-52, 54		
8:22	52	**1 Timothy**	
8:23	52	1:3–4	15
12:1	130	2:8–10	61
12:3	7n27	2:9	62
12:13	130	3:16	102n22
14	118	6:9–10	132
14:2–4	118	6:9–18	77
		6:17	76
1 Corinthians		6:18–19	62
3	50		
3:3–4	51	**Titus**	
3:21–23	51	2:2–6	61
8:5	51n9		
15:15	51n9	**Hebrews**	
		1:1–2	50
2 Corinthians		2:11	127
4:17	53	6:10	128
5:2–4	52	7:1–10	125
5:4	52	7:9	126
8:9	42	8:5	89n47
9:11	62	9	129n17,21
		9:9	89n47
Galatians		9:14	89n47
1:6–9	47	9–13	127n13, 129n17,21
1:8–9	15		
2:10	64	10:24	128
3:28	61	10:32	126, 128
		10:34	126
Ephesians		10:32–39	126
4:28	62	10:33–34	131
		10:34	132
Philippians		11:8	126
2:5–11	53	11:25–26	126
2:9	50	12:2	126
3:10	51, 53	13:1	129

13:1–6	121, 121n1, 126-127	3:14–22	81
		3:18	84n29
13:1–17	126	4	84
13:1	127n11	4:3	84, 92
13:2	127n11, 129	4:6	84
13:3	130	5:8	84
13:5	62, 127n11, 132-133	5:9	91n55-56
		5:9–10	89
13:6	133	5:12	84
13:13	54, 126	6:9–11	81n9
13:15	128	6:15	86n38, 91n54
13:16	128-129	6:15–17	69
		7:9	91n55
James		7:13–14	81n9
2:1–7	69	7:15	89
2:2	62, 75	8:3	84
		10:11	91n54
1 Peter		11:2	91n54
2:21	53	11:9	91n54
3:3–4	62	11:18	91n54
4:9	130	12:5	91n54
4:12–13	52n15	13:7	86n38, 91n54
		13:9–10	81n9
2 Peter		13:16	82n14
1:3–11	150	14	91n54
1:5	149	14:7	90
		15:3–4	91n55
3 John		15:4	90
5–8	130	15:6	84
		15:7	84
Revelation		16:9	91
1:6	89	16:12	91n54
1:9	81n9	16:14	86n38, 91n54
1:12–20	84	16:19	91n54
1–20	81	17	83n21
2:1–3:22	82n12	17:2	83, 91n54
2.6	81n10	17:4	82
2.8–11	81	17:6	81n9
2:9	82n12, 84n29	17:6b–7	84
2:9–10	81n9	17:12	91n54
2:14	81n10, 127	17:15	86n38, 91n54
2:15	81n10	17:18	91n54
2:20–25	81n10	17–18	82
2:27	91n54	17–22	83n21, 90
3:12	89	18	83n23, 25

18:3	91n54	Didache	
18:4–8	84	11–12	130
18:9	91n54	12.1	130
18:11–17	83, 93n62		
18:23	91n54	Testament of Joseph	
19:7	90	1:6	167
19:15	91n54	1:7	168
19:18	91n54	2:1	168
19:19	91n54	2:2	168
20:4	81n9	2:3a	168
20:6	89	3:3–4	168
20:8	86n38, 91n54	3:10	168
21	89-90	8:5	168
21:1–22:5	81, 85, 87, 88n42, 90n51, 91n56, 93	9:5	168
		11:6–7	168
21–22	85n34		
21:3	87-88		
21:8	85		
21:9	85		
21:11	92-93		
21:12–18	85		
21:15–17	88		
21:18	86, 92-93		
21:19–20	90n50		
21:19	92		
21:21	86, 93		
21:22	88		
21:23	92-93		
21:24	86, 91n56		
22:2	91n55		
22:3–4	89		
22:5	93		

3 Baruch
  11.9   149n20

1 Enoch
  14:20–21 92n59

2 Enoch
  65:8–10   92n59

Psalms of Solomon
  5.2   82n14

www.ingramcontent.com/pod-product-compliance
Lightning Source LLC
Chambersburg PA
CBHW050317120526
44592CB00014B/1943